MW00710914

To Gloria & Jim,

Thanks for your

friendship,

Ed Ruben

2/2/2013

Ed Rabel Reports: Lies, Wars and Other Misadventures

By
Ed Rabel

Keith Publications, LLC
www.keithpublications.com
©2012

Arizona
USA

Ed Rabel Reports:
Lies, Wars and Other Misadventures

Copyright© 2012

By Ed Rabel

Edited by Tamara Eaton
http://tamaraeatoneditingservices.weebly.com

Cover art by Elisa Elaine Luevanos
www.ladymaverick81.com

Cover art Keith Publications, LLC © 2012
www.keithpublications.com

ISBN: 978-1-936372-67-6

If you are interested in purchasing more works of this nature, please stop by
www.dinkwell.com

Contact information: info@keithpublications.com
Visit us at: www.keithpublications.com
Printed in The United States of America

3

Dedication

This book is dedicated to those who do not lie.
You know who you are.

Acknowledgements

I am grateful to everyone who helped make this book possible in ways both large and seemingly small, starting with my colleagues and producers at CBS and NBC. I can never adequately repay my producer at CBS Sunday Morning, James Houtrides, for sustaining me in every conceivable way through years of instruction about good story-telling and minimalist writing. We almost reached our goal of zero-based narration on television. I am sure I failed him herein as I rambled on and on in book form.

Drollene Plattner Brown, my editor and high school chum, was a wonderful sounding board and provided just the right amounts of encouragement, patience, understanding, and good judgment while steering this manuscript to publication. No one should hold her responsible for the conclusions I draw, particularly about our home state of West Virginia. The opinions are strictly my own. Thanks also to Drollene's sister, Sharon, for reading the manuscript to provide fresh eyes about bloody scenes like my grandfather's chicken-killing ways.

Tamara Eaton, my editor at Keith Publications, provided her highly professional touch to the manuscript. In her knowledgeable recommendations and precise excision, her joy in helping other writers improve shines through. I also appreciate the good work of Ray Dyson, my proofreader at Keith Publications, for his newsman's sensitivity to the voice of the writer.

My agent, Diane Nine, provided much needed advice, wise counsel, and encouragement from the inception of the idea for this book until the final manuscript and beyond.

I appreciate the encouragement of my colleagues and students at University School in Hunting Valley, Ohio and also value their support and introduction to the world of academia. A graduate of University School and my attorney, Timothy Koontz, is a stalwart ally and trusted advisor who provides inestimable guidance and financial assistance.

My friends and relatives in West Virginia encouraged me and bore with me throughout this project, often providing sound advice, but even more important, offering a refuge from the sometimes stressful and solitary work of writing a book. I'll only mention a few—my cousins, the Curry brothers, Randy, John, Todd and Clinton, and their mother Betty Rabel Curry—among the many who deserve recognition. Again, they bear no responsibility for the opinions expressed herein. But they do give me a deep understanding of the mountain culture and religiosity that permeate all of my West Virginia environs. I am especially grateful to Raymond Kandel, founder and former owner of WKLC in St. Albans without whom I would ever have chanced upon a truly marvelous, 50-year-long career in broadcasting.

Table of Contents

I
Becoming Ed Rabel

1
Blood, Guts and Ice Cream Sundaes

Those who cannot remember the past are condemned to repeat it.
—George Santayana

The stench of blood filled my nostrils, and frantic screams pierced my ears. It was nothing new, and neither was the sight of my grandfather in a thick leather apron that protected him and made him look like a monster ready to torture someone with myriad knives and other gleaming artifacts sharpened to the hilt. But the screaming came from a clawing cock. The blood spewed onto me and the ground, the cock's talons flexing to try to force freedom as granddad's gloved hands grasped, vice-like, the bird's neck and, in a blink-of-an-eye, life was cast out as the flapping corpse soared into a steel barrel, where it thrashed and bled itself to death. Even as a lad of six, I knew I would remember this, retain it and ponder it for future use.

The dead chicken and its cage mates were thrown into scalding water to do the final trick. The steel barrel overflowed with the steaming, boiling water, thick with feathers that would fly right off for the picking.

Grandpop gutted the headless fowl in front of me, and I watched the guts stream onto the bare earth on which I walked. My canvas shoes filled with blood that seeped out onto the floor even at bedtime. Redness blended into my cotton socks, which I took off when the sun went down and put right back on when the sun came up because Mom did not wash them. I will wear them into eternity.

A future of blood and guts awaited me in Vietnam, Cambodia, Laos, Nicaragua, Memphis, Baghdad, Jerusalem, Washington, D.C., Atlanta and many other horrifying places on the earth that see bloodbaths from time to time. But I didn't know it, yet.

Unbeknownst to me and buried now deeply in my subconscious, boyhood images of poverty and guilt were gluing themselves onto memory banks entitled "Non-ending." The memories never came unstuck, so I grew into adolescence and then into manhood bearing a burden that would not leave me alone. My child's brain precisely captured sights and sounds that stick with me and flash back in perfect recall. My eye was a camera recording vividly every moment of every day. Each of the perfectly stored moments was put on pause, to be replayed at will.

I can see myself, barely pubescent but seeking work, as I walked into Dr. Johnson's Drug Store over on the West Side of Charleston, West Virginia. A bell rang above the door, alerting soda jerks and pharmacists and other behind-the-counter laborers that a young Mr. Pineapple Face had arrived. A lack of good nutrition and the absence of a good upbringing caused me to walk slightly bent forward, my motion stymied by clumsiness. An aura of doubt surrounded me, something I did not perceive at the time, though everyone else must have. I remember feeling as though I competed with Abraham Lincoln, aiming for the ceiling, even though no stovepipe hat sat atop my head.

Nervously I glanced left and right to watch out for the bullies who might be there. Everyday bullies created a fear that consumed me. I couldn't come out of a candy store without one of them getting into my face. My jaw was slightly out of joint because one of them had sucker-punched me outside Stonewall Jackson High School, also on the West Side. Nobody counted for anything over there on the West Side except those who lived on top of the hill. But I was from the wrong hill, where my grandfather slaughtered chickens and candled eggs for sale by testing them against a bright light.

I mopped the floor of the drugstore in my new job, a 13-year-old clasping proudly my new Social Security card xxx-xx-1045. A flashback mingles strong-smelling bleach from the mop with a malodorous, bloody grandpa who grimaced as the birds tried out their razor sharp talons on him. A close-up focuses on Grandpop's yellow-stained false teeth protruding between strained lips, which showed either a snarl or a smile.

The memory continues: "You sure do look a lot like your grandpa," a could-be father-in-law said. He bestowed the unflattering remark with a smarmy leer that reaffirmed the skinny boy should keep hands off the daughter. "Your grandpa buys chickens and eggs off of me," he said, lumping me in with all the other ne'er-do-wells trying to get into June Ann's panties. I despaired over being lumped in. I emerged, but without June Ann.

Mopping up was not my only duty at the drugstore. I jerked up milkshakes and sodas and vanilla cokes for thirsty folks who leafed through Superman and Batman and The Green Hornet, the characters perched on dark, stained shelves at eye level, their capes and masks beguiling the Saturday afternoon crowd. White marble-top tables hid shaky knees, touching skittishly, as the teenagers began the eternal tango that keeps the world alive.

I knew about sex, but I hid my knowledge. Forbidden fruit sat on those red cushioned bar stools that stood at attention to welcome the sundry guests. Behind the counter my hormones ran with a wild crowd—except there were no wild crowds. The currency of the day was pretense. I smiled my toothy grin at the forbidden and put my chocolate where it was supposed to be, in tall glasses filled with ice creams, bubbles, whipped creams and a cherry. I served those flighty girls in bobby socks, saddle shoes and crinolines, as they jumped for joy even before Elvis gyrated into their lives.

The bell above the door rang, and a sheepish man walked in. Tiptoeing to the counter, he asked me conspiratorially to sell him a box of balloons. I knew perfectly well what they were and where they were kept hidden. I had even opened one of the packages and tried one of them on for size. One size does not fit all. They were under the counter, of course. Not out in the open on racks and in the movies and in public toilets and on the Internet and via texting and on Mom and Dad's bed, and during a "nooner" and out in the open and in your face. Everything about you-know-what was kept under the counter.

The apertures in my wide eyes opened fully. So did my mouth. "Come on, boy," the hangdog whispered. "Gimme some balloons. Come on."

Hormones, dread, excitement, anxiety, bashfulness—everything one can imagine—filled my gangly being as I wondered, *What am I going to do*? And I did what any goofball would do at a time like this; I shouted at the top of my lungs, "Hey, Dr. Johnson! Do we have any balloons?"

There were no repercussions after that scene. No, the denouement of my drugstore career was something else. I see it yet, the incident that was my downfall. I peddled the drugstore bicycle through dark streets and up Magazine Hollow to deliver a prescription. I zoomed across pathways and alleyways and plowed through lanes that would be inundated one day with wet human bodies and drowned-out houses in the worst gully-washer Charleston ever experienced. I climbed hundreds of stairs to the shack. A fat old woman moaned on a couch just beneath a stark light bulb giving little light. My eye was in full record mode. The man of the house stood in the doorway, holding out his hand to receive the delivery.

"That will be $13.20, sir," I said, my ears trying to ignore the sound of the woman's moans.

"I thought Dr. Litton was gonna take care of that," Doorman replied.

A shriveled supplicant, I murmured, "Oh, okay," and I handed the drugs to Shackman, who slammed the rickety door in my pallid face.

Dogs growled as I peddled back to Dr. Johnson's Drug Store, wondering whether I have fulfilled my mission. *Let's see, what was it Dr. Johnson said?* The question floated up to the front of my mind, then receded, coming over and over, the same thought 'til day's end. And the answer was always the same.

"No, boy, you messed up. You were supposed to get the money and if not, bring the medicine back here." I had known that all along, of course. But even as a stripling I knew I shouldn't leave anybody in the lurch. This I knew if I knew nothing else. And for my good intentions I was fired.

I thought of the shamefaced fellow who had asked for balloons, remembered him as he returned to his pocket the fifty-cent coin he had squirreled away to buy a three-pack of Trojans. I could see him slink out of the store empty-handed, letting the bell clang behind him. And I, the

14

reluctant youngster, my counterfeit innocence intact, had gone on about my business in a dark corner someplace, giving it a go.

Whenever it happened—and it didn't happen often for me, actually never until I was 18—it was in the back seat of a car or at the drive-in picture show. And usually in the dark. I learned early girls didn't like to do it in daylight or in lamplight or even in moonlight. "Turn off the light," she would say. "Uh, could we put some sheets over us?" the pouty maiden implored. "How about let's get really drunk and then do it," the horny girl pleaded. "Okay?"

I finally figured it out, genius that I am. The girls wanted plausible deniability. In the cool of the morning when bras and panties were back in place concealing private parts no longer privatized, and sweaters and crinolines covering turgescence, and newly applied war paint enhancing the baby blues, she could say, "Uh, uh. Nope, that didn't happen. Em, em, em, I didn't pee in the snowdrift. Not nunna me. Snow White didn't drift. Gotta go home now. Just take me home where it will be yesterday all over again." In hindsight, the man sees the duplicity as outlandishly charming. At the time, though, the boy, in mighty amazement, was left holding his wonderment in his hand.

The boy could little guess that in a bit more than a decade's time, the man would be far from the mountains and valleys of Charleston, West Virginia, living in a land of concrete canyons. Today, the camera is still rolling to make sure the boy doesn't miss anything.

15

2
Angst and Discovery

Falsehood has an infinity of combinations, but truth has only one mode of being.
—Jean-Jacques Rousseau

Following my stint as a 13-year-old soda jerk, at 14 I became an usher at the Kearse Theater in Charleston. I saw all the movies multiple times, but one of my favorites was *South Pacific*. I watched the love stories play out, and it became my fantasy that I would one day find my own Liat out there in the world, somewhere outside the mountains I was coming to define as my prison.

I dutifully completed grades 9, 10, 11 and 12. My family's move from Charleston to St. Albans during my junior year in high school was significant for me at the time, getting me away from the bullies at Stonewall Jackson High to more civilized territory. My new classmates welcomed me, and I carved out a perfect niche. Mine was the voice of the school's new radio program, "St. Albans High School is on the Air." I shared dreams and ambitions with my classmates, but aside from some puppy love with a blond bombshell/cheerleader/class president, there is nothing much more to report about my high school days. She got away and married a SEAL.

Except there is more to report. At the time it was the most astounding thing in the world. A black boy entered my class. He was a boy and he was black—the first black ever to attend St. Albans High School. His name was James Brown, a name that will live forever in the hearts and minds of his all-white classmates. Just a year or so after *Brown v.*

Board of Education, the landmark United States Supreme Court case in which the court declared state laws segregating schools unconstitutional, my school was forced to integrate. James Brown was, therefore, an oddity. But he was not an outcast. He integrated peacefully, without rancor. In fact, he became a star in our class. His specialness struck me at the time. And his being captured my imagination and helped identify my own humanity for all time. For, you see, I grew up in a racist family. When black sanitation workers came to collect the garbage in my neighborhood, my mother, otherwise a kind and gentle woman, ordered me indoors because, she shouted, "The niggers are coming, the niggers are coming."

A child of my age did not know the meaning of being appalled. Loving mothers, after all, always knew best, didn't they? Still, even then, there came a churning in my stomach and in my unconscious soul that something was wrong despite the neighborhood covenant, "you ain't nothin' but a jigaboo, boy," was as common as summertime flies. Although my kith and kin seldom saw an African-American in our lily-white localities, it did not prevent the prevalence of Negro-bashing in my region. Our elders were to blame. Racism was in their genes, implanted long ago and kept alive to be passed down from generation to generation as a shibboleth unquestioned, although I began questioning it. A child does not reason out racism as a puzzlement, for puzzlement is not in his vocabulary. But he does look around in wonder, though wonder in its adultness eludes him. A fundamental human struggle against the epochs of evil stirs within the child … if he is lucky. Yet he will be taunted by his peers for his uncommon zeal, which must be lugged along over time to emerge fully formed as an outlandish call-to-arms. I cured myself of the disease in its early stages, knowing even then it was debilitating and ultimately lethal. And so it was as the boy introduced himself, unencumbered by the racism of his past, to take

17

up the common campaign for civil rights alongside the blacks he never knew.

When James Brown came to school we knew the blacks were coming. In spearheading the charge, James changed our racist minds forevermore. My encounter with the war of words began in the halls of my high school. My good experience with this first, positive encounter with race shaped my attitudes and marked my mind-set to challenge racism and racists wherever I found them. Thank you, James.

Morris Harvey College on the banks of the Kanawha River did what she could to show me the way, to know the veracity of things. My alma mater's motto: "Ye shall know the truth and the truth shall set you free." John 8:32. The truth was my most instructive tutors were at the local radio and TV stations, where I worked full time while going to college.

About that time I was an Elvis Presley look-alike in full acne array wearing long black trousers, narrow white belts and high-collared black shirts. My GI haircut on top and ducktails along the sides were kept strictly obedient with Lucky Tiger Butch Hair Wax, which I received free of charge for flogging the gooey glue on the air. At 145 pounds soaking wet, I looked like a victim of tuberculosis, with eyes sunken and teeth an uneven fence. I gave a great impression of a scarecrow, stringy tall at six feet, three inches.

I started my broadcast career in St. Albans at WKLC, 13-hundred on your dial, lucky for listening. Not yet dry behind the ears at age 15, I gathered a big audience of teens who liked "Ed Rabel on the turntable." You see, back then, we actually played records on turntables … never mind. By the time I was 18, I was working at WHMS, 1490 on your dial, in Charleston, and my popularity among teens had soared, landing a big, fat contract for the radio station. "Slip me some skin, Jackson," the long, tall beatnik would say. I offered the fifties version of a fist-bump by extending my hand, palm up. I would have to wait a few more years if I wanted to become a hippie. For now, beatnik would have to do.

Little Richard, Elvis Presley and I were hot! And that terminology hadn't been invented yet. PR agency McCann-Erikson told the makers of Gillette Blue Blades that teenagers in the Kanawha Valley had gone batty over my very hip show, number one on the ratings chart. McCann-Erikson's survey showed the "Rabel-rouser" was on a roll.

Teens tuned in by the thousands to listen to "Rabelious." Gillette so liked my style they agreed to let me simply ad-lib the spots I would do for them. No scripts, little control. Big mistake. Big, big mistake.

McCann-Erikson knew I was outrageous and unpredictable—nay, reckless—on the air. That was part of the charm of an 18-year-old smart-ass. Still, the agency was willing to take a chance in its campaign to suck kids in, get 'em hooked early on the blade of choice. But they kept a close eye on me.

A representative of the PR firm came to town, unannounced, checked into a hotel and listened in on my performance. I was deep into my very clever banter about how youngsters should start shaving with Blue Blades. But there were other uses for the exceptionally sharp blades, weren't there? Of course, idiot answered.

These words came right out of my addle-pated, teen-age brain, into my mouth, through my lips, into the microphone and instantly onto the ears of vast legions of my fans, not to

19

mention the agent hiding in that hotel room with her radio turned on.

"...and if it is *suicide* you're considering this fine morning, do it right with Gillette Blue Blades. You can't go wrong if you use these new blades to slash your wrists." Clearly I was, at that time, a jock about to invent shock radio.

The agent's critique was miraculously muted. "You were terrific, but in the future just omit the part about suicide."

The radio station kept its contract and I kept my job, but my self-destructive behavior had a life of its own. *I'll jump from a bridge ... or just shoot myself,* I thought. There was more than one way to break out.

3
Mountain Anthems

Is not this the true romantic feeling - not to desire to escape life,
but to prevent life from escaping you?
—Thomas Wolfe

I can't go on without reminiscing about my startup at WKLC in St. Albans. Wall-to-wall Elmer Gantrys populated the studios. The preachers used the station's microphones to beg for money, promising nothing but the fear of God in return. A faith healer named Dr. Paul Collett offered to "build the biggest tabernacle in West Virginia," and multitudinous collections came pouring in. Dr. Collett, himself, skipped town with his suitcases filled with the suckers' hard-earned money. Afterward his once-gullible supporters, those who'd sent him their last dollars, warned everybody that "Dr. Collett wants your wallet!" He surely did.

The anthems of the mountains radiated off the station's transmission tower. Up the smoky hollows and along the streams polluted by the residue of coal mining, radios fed the raw-boned inhabitants their daily diet of the elemental gospels and *Deliverance* banjo tunes they regarded as music to their ears. "Creekers" inside doublewides clinging to creek banks longed for a John Denver to glorify their meager surroundings with a song of praise called "Almost Heaven, West Virginia."

The hymn would become a worldwide smash hit that conjured images of a proud people living nicely between and on top of mountains surrounded by breathtaking beauty. The need to go home was the melody's overriding theme. *Life older than the trees ... younger than the mountains ...Country roads, take me home.*

But my own internal plea was escape, not revalidation. I knew the ugly truth about West Virginia and southern Appalachia that John Denver would one day gloss over with charming sappiness. Lack of opportunity, provincialism, traditionalism, fatalism and religious fundamentalism were omnipresent in my neighborhood. Stagnation and corruption were rampant. Anti-intellectualism was pervasive.

Some may argue my memory stereotypes my people and my region without scientific evidence for support. I tell them experiential proof is good enough for me. Then, as now, I knew *poverty stricken* when I saw it. I was personally acquainted with the destitution farmers suffered when their subsistence farms went out of date. My instincts told me the dole was a way of life. Depression and depressives filled up the funeral homes of my existence.

Extracting coal, the prime industry, became a matter for machines, casting jobless miners into their own coal dust. An attitude of resignation permeated a populace begging God to take them home for the ultimate release from the hell of their tormented lives here on mountain earth. This place was—and is—a mining colony on the moon waiting for the mines to play out.

Somehow I knew at an early age that homegrown sectarianism, by any other name, was likely to capture me. I sensed, intuitively and fearfully, that for the success of their own religious project, the "saved" were insisting their internal opponents must be either purged or salvaged. I therefore launched my exit strategy.

22

Almost as soon as I turned on my microphone at WKLC I began to broadcast distress signals from my radio perch. The station owner and operator, Ray Kandel, heard my cries, took in the waif and pulled the urchin out of his blind sanctuary to reveal a world of possibilities. To my benefactor, Kandel, I shall be indebted for all time.

Later, following my stint at WHMS, another station in Charleston hired me for more money and better hours. But at WCAW I had to work with a crow. Matie the crow flew out of her cage into my hair. I had hair then. She defecated all over the place. She jumped on the turntables and scratched the records, 33 1/3 long-playing vinyl recordings. "Caw! Caw! Caw!" screeched the crow right out into the ether. *Let me out! Let me out! Let me out!* That was my inner squawking, constantly, without end.

Maybe President Harry Truman was trying to make a fast exit, too, when I caught up with him at Kanawha Airport. By then I was a local TV reporter. As a past president, Truman had come to Charleston to deliver a speech. I was stunned by Truman's lack of geographic acumen. He told me, on camera, how nice it was to be in Virginia. When I pointed out to him that he was in West Virginia, Truman didn't miss a beat. "Well, it should have been Virginia," he blurted.

For a lot of people outside the state, West Virginia doesn't exist. Asked what part of the country you're from, you answer correctly: "Oh, I'm from Charleston." "That's in South Carolina, isn't it?" the interlocutors respond. Or after hearing you say you're from West Virginia they will comment, "I have a cousin who lives in Richmond." Our statehood is oft denied by people who should know better. Perhaps the absence of definition prompted me to want to blast off many, many years ago.

When you are in it, you may not know your experience is a crucible. Sometimes you have no idea the events of the day prepare or doom you for all your days to come. The hard part is recognizing the important events and discarding all the rest. Some people wouldn't recognize an opportunity if it slapped them in the face. Others embrace failures as if they were the waves of the future and, by doing so, ruin themselves forevermore. Fortunately, I was perceptive.

I lived at home with my parents in a St. Albans subdivision called River Lake Estates while pursuing my radio and TV career—attending high school and then college. The move from downtown St. Albans—was a step up for the family, but it did not mitigate my urge to escape the hills that felt like a trap to me.

One fateful morning the sun came up right on time. My car bucked violently as I drove it through my subdivision over deep pot holes in the road. A short distance on, the car resisted like a rented mule. *Clunk, clunk, clunk* went its heartstrings. *Thump, thump, thump* went my tail. Then a light bulb flickered on in my tiny brain. Flickering turned into a blaze that sparked an explosion of anger and hopelessness and spawned a fiendish idea.

 A plan of unbelievable size and scope materialized. My plot was absolutely brilliant. Some evil men in my subdivision would not know what hit them.

Oh, you poor rascals, you evil doers commissioned to keep up the roads. You are about to get your just desserts for your unmentionable crimes of the roadway. You are marked, you who have ignored the repeated complaints of the subdivision's residents irate over their rutted roads. You greedy guys, you time-wasters, you who thumb your noses

24

at the long-suffering inhabitants. I am about to fix you, I hooted to myself.

On my morning drive-time radio show, I brought up the hole mess. Vivid were my descriptions of the potholed streets. Then I implored my faithful out there in WHMS radio land to listen carefully for the scoop I was about to transmit.

"This morning," I announced, "I tried to get out of River Lake Estates, where I reside, to come here to work. Potholes got in my way. Deep, bottomless pits in which automobiles and little animals have gone missing. As you know, I am a Boy Scout, and I came prepared."

I was just getting started. "When my car got stuck in one of the openings this morning I removed the step ladder I keep atop my car for just such emergencies and, with great effort, climbed out of the yawning crater." *That ought to do it*, I said to myself.

My father put the phone to his ear to take the call from the furious caretakers of River Lake Estates. "Did you hear what your goofy son said on his show this morning? We're gonna sue you and him for everything you have."

What we had wasn't much after all the auto repair bills from encounters with the great abysses in the road. My father conceded I had stretched the truth a little, well … actually a lot. But defending me, he pointed out that I had told the truth, basically. There was a pause on the other end of the line and then, *click*.

The next day swarms of blacktop trucks moved into River Lake Estates for the facelift. From then on the roads out of my subdivision were as smooth as melted butter. Forevermore the house where I lived with Dad, Mom, my younger sister and my older brother would be a shrine to that kid who got the roads repaired.

My successful foray into aggressive journalism told me something. My words were as powerful as lightning strikes. A young, impressionable correspondent realized his lingo, spoken truthfully, could, like the pen, be mightier than the sword. Keyed up by the idea, I jumped at the notion I could become a network television news correspondent. My grand mission was to rip off the mask of wrongdoers everywhere, put it on TV and assert truthfulness.

That was a noble vocation, guaranteed by our Constitution. And that's how it was in the early '60s, before America lost a war and gave up her virginity.

4
Innocence Lost

Truth uncompromisingly told will have its jagged edges.
—Herman Melville, *Billy Budd*

Intoxicating innocence turned to blatant soberness. Subsequent years of eye-popping change robbed me of my childlike thinking. In television's first war, in combat here and there, in intra-network skirmishes, truth was only a rumor, and doubt was a stranger I would encounter time after time. If I had been the suave, urbane man who's writing today, I would have dismissed outright the possibility of achieving the dream.

About the time Kennedy was killed, my big chance suddenly materialized. From small town radio I crossed the street and walked through the doors of Channel 8, WCHS-TV, and the CBS affiliate in Charleston. Ed Rabel on the turntable was now Ed Rabel on the TV news. News director, no less.

 The first order of business was to hire a reporter. The station was so cheap nobody I interviewed would work for the wages management authorized me to offer. I finally hired Don Fannin away from UPI for $110 a week, $10 more than I was earning.

I hired Don not just for his formidable journalistic skill, but also because he was entertaining. A story he told tickled my funny bone. Don said he had been sitting innocently at a bar in town when the female bartender, not of his acquaintance, approached and whispered in his ear: "I thought you ought to know," she murmured

27

conspiratorially. "Doreen got her tests back. She ain't got no clap." Doreen was not of Don's acquaintance, either. Oh, how I long for those days. Um … not really.

WCHS-TV was my escape pod, the medium I used to escape the psychosis brought on by my isolated mountain environment.

CBS News was looking for reporters to fill the ranks of its rapidly expanding news division. Walter Cronkite's evening newscast had just emerged from a black and white, fifteen-minute offering to a full thirty minutes "in living color." An entire half hour was devoted to network news. Can you imagine that? Unheard of. William Paley was spending hundreds of millions to make his the Tiffany Network. I was in the right place at the right time. CBS spotted me for full time work because of the stories I free-lanced and reported for them, on-air, from Appalachia. I was cool with that.

In Fayette County, for example, the disharmony caused by holy rollers dancing and speaking in tongues was the core of my documentary about serpent handling in my news bailiwick. The Reverend Elzie Priest hailed the coming of religious ruin for the "unsaved," while congregants made loud, unintelligible sounds of glossolalia as they worked themselves up into fits of erótica. Their ecstatic utterances terrified the lethal rattlers and copperheads that slithered over gnarled hands and wrinkled necks, while infants gazed, mesmerized, at their parents' thrashing from high, overhead perches along the walls. A single, bare, 40-watt light bulb hung from bald wires extending from the ceiling, where gruesome shadows played ominously. These true reflections of lunacy engulfed the fetid, packed little church house reeking of foul armpits and other unwashed body parts.

Pentecostalism, emphasizing the experience of Spirit baptism, gripped the sordid men and women. They drank strychnine from Mason jars that usually contained moonshine when not in use as containers to preserve green beans, corn and other food stuffs laid up for winter. The babel, combined with other dark rituals of the mountains' indigenous populace, lent credence to outside views that time had overlooked this place. Seen as unholy acts by strangers, the Acts of the Apostles were summoned by the religious fanatics as rightful reasons for their uncommon behavior. But left to their own devices, these people and their brethren were at risk of becoming obsolete in a world fascinated by progress. Worshippers who believe God will save them when the snake bites are truly out of their minds. God didn't invent free will for nothing.

> *For as the sowing, so the reaping*
> *Is now and evermore shall be*
> *Thou art delivered to thine own keeping*
> *Only thyself hath afflicted thee.*
> —Rudyard Kipling, *Natural Theology*

There were female religionists who wouldn't cut their hair and refused to wear lipstick out of the fear of God. One evangelical woman I knew wanted to get it on with an Episcopal minister, but his moderate consumption of alcohol from time to time and his occasional use of dirty words threatened to spoil the relationship. Maybe she was right in letting him go, but it was the perception *she* was wrong that did her in. As much as we don't like the box others construct for us, we are stuck in there because we don't want to change our ways. Some call that courage. Others call it quits.

"Free at last, free at last, thank God Almighty, I'm free at last!" The motto of the American Negroes' movement to break out of their racial prisons served me just as well for the great escape from my mountain detention in 1966. I was giddy. I was sad. I was exhilarated. I was tormented. In all, I was triumphant. The great American promises of just rewards for hard work and perseverance paid off back then. Champagne in first class reaffirmed the dream came true. Even if I had known then I was the perfect cliché, I would have rejected the notion outright. This was good and it was true. On my way to CBS News in New York, at high altitude I watched the mountainous ridges recede, their alabaster eternity glistening beneath tall, green pines that lent credence to the truism of West Virginia's highland majesty. Despite the natural beauty of the place, though, the cord was cut. Make no mistake. I was glad to get out. Yet, there was a sadness about my departure. Foothill vibrance gave way to various shades of azure, which turned even darker green and ultimately into blackness so unyielding I was sure this was a blackout. *There was no going back.* My history closed its door on me, erasing itself, cutting me off for my own good and throwing me into the icy cold water of future. I began to shiver as I said to myself, *Farewell.*

5
Out of the Hills
… and into urban canyons

Knock, knock, knock. "Police," whispered a voice on the other side of my Manhattan apartment door. *Oh, okay*, I thought as I opened the entrance. Fearsome men in black turtlenecks stood there, pistols drawn and poised to brush past me when I said, "Show me some credentials." The leader of the men in black rolled his eyes skyward and produced his badge. "Come in," I said, as innocently as any other country boy might who is new to the big city.

"Turn off your TV and the lights," the leader ordered. His two-way radio chattered, and as I rushed around turning off the TV and lights, I focused on the voices coming through the radio. "Okay, he's on the ladder. Okay, he's about to go through the window. Okay, he's inside. Go! Go! Go!" All the turtlenecks ran out onto my patio.

I learned later that several women on my floor had been raped by a serial rapist, and a trap had been set to lure him into the next door apartment and to kill him as he fled, thus bringing swift justice without a court order. They'd removed the woman who rented the apartment, putting in her place a female police officer who knew karate and was dressed in skimpy lingerie. To help lure the quarry into the apartment, the police had opened a window and put sharp scissors in plain sight.

The policewoman lounged seductively on a sofa. Madman jumped through the open window, grabbed the scissors and pounced on her before two detectives hiding in another room could react. She screamed. "Get off of me, get off of me!" One of the detectives finally pulled the enraged man

31

off the flailing female, whose karate had failed her. The other detective confronted the man and deliberately fired his .38 special into the criminal's chest. The bullet raced through shirt, skin and innards, and emerged at supersonic speed, slamming into the detective who'd been holding the rapist so his partner could get a good shot. The wounded officer stumbled into the hallway and slowly crumbled, bleeding profusely. Ignoring the injured rapist, the police went to the aid of their friend.

The officer in charge asked frantically to use my phone to call an ambulance. He dialed a number and waited and waited. No answer. "Just like New York City," he said. "You never can get the police when you need them." No one is neighborly in The City.

This was my introduction to the big time. Both the villain and the policeman survived their wounds. But the rapist went free because the police used entrapment in their mission to execute him. *Only in New York*, I thought. Just a few days into my brand new way of life, all the way from the comforts and coziness and consistency of home in rural West Virginia, and my being was turned upside down. The baptism under fire had begun. Life was giving me a taste test of mortality I had not experienced before. There would be countless encounters with the trouble of humanity. The war of words with life and death came up over and over again during the next three decades as I worked as an on-air correspondent for both CBS and NBC.

II
Sons of the South

6
Against all Odds

A man's worth is no greater than the worth of his ambitions.
—Marcus Aurelius

CBS News assigned me to its bureau in Atlanta not long after the shooting in New York. Violence was bloodying Martin Luther King's non-violence with water hoses and attack dogs and gunfire that painted the struggle for civil rights over the entire south. In the words of my favorite author, Pat Conroy, I was all "white knuckles and white flags, signaling surrender at every turn."

Having grown up in the south did make the new assignment ideal for me and for CBS. The south was familiar territory. Maybe I could avoid another hair-raising New York style episode on the turf I knew so well. *Surely you jest*, my more cogent side intoned. I knew going in we had suppressed some of the racism that had long besieged America from its founding. While George Washington led the troops against the British and Thomas Jefferson laid down the law for all time, slavery was already the colonial trademark. I also knew we had a long way to go. Racial discrimination still churned above and below the patina of modern civilization. In 1967, America was torn by racism still.

Right wing extremists and "know-nothings" and other anti-intellectuals had used hate language all along. But Alabama Governor George Wallace cornered the market in his early campaigns to degrade black people. I remember it well. He was one of the first of a long line of racists I would confront in on-camera interviews.

I was one of those "slick-haired Yankee newsmen," in Wallace's parlance, who came to the south to "ruin" southerners' way of life. Never mind that I was from West Virginia and balding. He attacked us with his malevolent words.

When Wallace lost an early election for governor, he told his campaign aide in no uncertain terms his future battles would be infamous for his barefaced and coarsest use of English so nobody would misunderstand him. From now on, he said, "I am going to put the feed right down there where the hogs can get at it." His aide, Seymore Trammell, recalled Wallace saying, "Seymore, you know why I lost that governor's race? I was out niggered…and I'll tell you here and now, I will never be out niggered again." The grubby, populist theme worked. He was elected governor in 1963 and went on to serve three successive terms in the high office. In his first inaugural, Wallace pronounced, "Segregation now and segregation forever."

By the time he ran for president, Wallace had moderated his racial stance somewhat, but his history was replete with the spikes of bigotry. He was a small man in stature and worth, and his little feet filled teeny shoes that echoed tap, tap, tap, everywhere he went.

Pugnacious to a fault, the former boxer's smile looked like the permanent, petulant frown that usually enveloped his visage. His sneer was the epitome of his public and private dealings. Wallace is remembered best, perhaps, for his bullying posture in the schoolhouse door. In 1963 he blocked two black students who were trying to register at the University of Alabama. In full view of national and international news cameras, Wallace stood at the entrance of the university declaring Alabama's right to run its schools the way it wanted, segregated.

Deputy U.S. Attorney General Nicholas Katzenbach waited patiently for Wallace to come to the end of his speech. Then, backed up by national guardsmen, Katzenbach watched Wallace step aside to abide by a federal court order to end the university's segregation. The populist, segregationist stand served him well. In 1968 he ran for president as a third party candidate, winning five states and 46 electoral votes.

A skirt chaser, Wallace intimidated his wife by flaunting his indiscretions and forcing her to attend his political rallies while she was in extreme pain, dying of cancer.

Wallace was gunned down during his race for the presidency. The bullet damaged his spine, paralyzing him from the waist down. Those who hated him, and they were legion, took pleasure in knowing he could never successfully engage in sexual intercourse again.

But while Wallace was still on his feet, his audiences responded positively to his viciousness by using their fists and throwing chairs and invectives at me and the other reporters assigned to cover him. Unleashing the attack dogs against the media worked as well then as it does today.

In the words of many segregationists like Wallace, CBS was the "Communist Broadcasting System," NBC was the "Nigger Broadcasting Company," and ABC the "African Broadcasting Company." What an encounter with the trouble of humanity.

7
For Everyone There is a Season

*We may have all come on different ships, but we're in the
same boat now.*
—Martin Luther King Jr.

In that repulsive environment in 1968, Martin Luther King
arrived in Memphis, Tennessee, to bolster garbage men
striking for better pay. My veteran cameraman, Laurens
Pierce, and I watched and recorded Dr. King as he made a
dark speech. It would be his last public address.

"Mine eyes have seen the glory of the coming of the Lord!"
Those were the last words of the final speech, the haunting
finale of a lifetime of resistance. Pierce recorded those
words for posterity. Pierce would go on to be the lone
cameraman to shoot the footage of Governor Wallace
being shot down in a shopping center parking lot.

Now he was filming King's speech, which was replete with
references to death—King recounting some of the many
times he had faced mortality during his non-violent
campaign.

"There was the time in Harlem," he said, "when a
demented black woman stabbed me in the chest with an
ice pick as I was signing my first book during a book
signing event. The blade," he said, "was touching my aorta.
The doctors told me that if I had so much as sneezed I
would have died."

Pierce turned to me and said, "You must see to it that this
gets on the air. It is prophetic." Pierce had never before

heard or filmed King speaking like this, about life and death, about his life and his brushes with death. Nor had I. The speech would get on the air incessantly in the days to come. We were within hours of the excruciating moment in Memphis when an assassin would gun down the messenger of peace and non-violence. How lucky America was to have him, a man of peace, in that place and time. If the Rap Browns and the Stokely Carmichaels of the movement had prevailed with their bare-fisted confrontations with white America, there is no telling how deep the racial divide would have become.

For months we witnessed Dr. King as he used Gandhi's philosophy to disarm the haters who wanted him to die. Now he was in a city seething with the odium that divides us to this day. In the year of our Lord 1968, Memphis, whose namesake is the ancient capital of the godlike pharaohs of Egypt, would begin to curse itself forever as the hometown of horror where the King was killed.

Just hours before he was assassinated at the Lorraine Motel in the heart of Memphis, Dr. King let me interview him on-camera. I may have been the last reporter ever to put questions to him formally. He showed up for the interview bearing his message of hope and peace. "The arc of the moral universe is long," he repeated, "but it bends toward justice."

This was a towering, awesome figure to the very end. He was also a witty and mischievous man caught by my camera in the parking lot of the place he would be killed. A federal marshal handed Dr. King an order forbidding the protest march he had pledged to lead. The marshal stood in front of King, who pretended to read the order solemnly.

Then Dr. King called to his aides: "Andy, come over here." Andrew Young, who would later become ambassador to the U.N. under President Jimmy Carter, walked to King's side. "Reverend Orange, come over here," said Dr. King, a smile playing on his lips. "Ralph, come look at this," he said to his number two, Ralph Abernathy. "Jesse," he motioned to a very young Jesse Jackson in bibbed overalls. All gathered around and looked at the marshal in mock earnestness. Then, Dr. King made his proclamation: "This injunction says we can't march on Monday. Well, we gonna give this injunction to our attorneys. We don't have time for such orders. We have some marchin' to do!" Everyone, including the U.S. marshal broke into laughter.

Mayor Henry Loeb, on the other hand, was a somber man. The mayor of Memphis was so grim he nearly made himself believable. Appearing in his office for our on-camera interview, Loeb had a shotgun at his side. I thought he had lost his sanity. Loeb was all anger and vinegar, blustering and forewarning, alarming and threatening. He would allow no lawlessness. And his mounted police would back him up.

The brutal breakup of King's first protest march for the Memphis sanitation workers was proof of Loeb's mean promise. Some of King's followers smashed store windows along the parade route. King, horrified, was whisked away. Loeb's pony soldiers, meanwhile, swung their clubs and spurred their horses, herding black people brutally back into their neighborhoods to be bludgeoned unmercifully.

Chagrined by the violence, King vowed to lead a peaceful protest the following week. He would not live long enough to do so.

King's peaceful movement wiped out most of the vestiges of segregation in the South. His fight for economic justice in America was far more complicated and much less successful than his struggle for human rights. The frustrations put him in a bad mood, which reduced his effectiveness as his self-proclaimed "Drum Major for Justice."

In a word, King was depressed. He planned not to go to Memphis in the first place. He was under pressure from President Johnson for his public opposition to the war in Vietnam where poor black men, underprivileged white men and deprived Hispanics bore the brunt of the fighting. Forty years later, many of the sons and daughters of America's disfavored are laying down their lives in Afghanistan.

King's noble stance led to passage of the Civil Rights Act of 1964 that abolished legal segregation. The Voting Rights Act was passed in 1965. King fought to the death against economic disparity. The fight was flagging when his assassin struck.

James Earl Ray was the lone gunman, in my opinion. Nobody wants to believe a lowly loser like Ray could transform history so dramatically on his own. He had to have had help, so the thinking goes. I doubt it.

I went to Brushy Mountain State Prison in Tennessee to interview Ray on camera. He was locked up for life after confessing to the murder in order to escape execution by the state. Almost immediately he recanted. I wanted to know why.

In 1973 Al Gore, the future vice president of the United States, and I traveled as a team to conduct the interview. Gore was an investigative reporter then for *The Tennessean*, a position he held from 1971 to 1976. During the two-hour drive from Memphis to the prison, Gore never cracked a smile.

Perhaps I bored him. I don't know. All I know is he was extremely focused and deliberate. As fiercely as I wanted to get at the truth about the murderer, Gore was doubly fierce. He had not yet invented the Internet, but he was well on his way.

As my camera crew set up for the interrogation, Gore prepped me. He was steeped in the facts and rumors that surrounded the case. I had covered Ray's trial during which he confessed. Later, Ray escaped from the Brushy Mountain prison only to be captured hiding under some leaves nearby.

Bloodhounds led the captors to his hiding place. Asked what Ray had to say for himself when he was brought in, the prison spokeswoman told me this: "I asked Ray what he had done," she said. "He said, 'I went out.' 'What did you do [while you were out]?' I asked. 'Nothin,' he replied." She wasn't much help.

Whether Ray expected assistance once outside was never determined. Speculation had it that Ray had friends, co-conspirators, who agreed to use a helicopter to fetch him after his escape. The truth: Ray was an escape artist. There was no helicopter; no associates could be found. Ray escaped on his own, but only for a few hours.

He had broken out of other prisons before. This time he enlisted his fellow inmates to create a diversion in the exercise yard. Ray fashioned a ladder out of plumbing pipes and simply climbed over the prison wall while the guards were busy stopping a fight his fellows staged.

Ray declined to reveal to Gore and me details of his escape. Gore hit him with one set of inquiries while I readied to hammer him with another volley of interrogations. Gore on the right, Rabel on the left, camera nailing Ray no matter which way he turned. Gore was

41

fiercely adamant, allowing no quarter, battering the killer with facts that eradicated the nonsense Ray used as his defense.

In the end, Gore ripped Ray to shreds, assailing his fabrications to such an extent that Ray fell back on repeating, "I am innocent, a fall guy. Someone named 'Raoul' in New Orleans paid me to be in Memphis when King was killed." But that story did not fly. Nor did any of his accounts about his role in the assassination bear any merit. Apparently Ray was creating doubts out of whole cloth. We do know, however, that Ray came from a family long known for racism. He expected George Wallace to be elected president. Wallace would then pardon Ray, he thought. Ray was delusional at least, insane at best. He died in prison in 1998, declaring his innocence to the end.

8
To Be or Not to Be

… that is the question: Whether 'tis Nobler in the mind
to suffer the Slings and Arrows of outrageous Fortune,
or to take Arms against a Sea of troubles,
and by opposing end them.
—William Shakespeare, *Hamlet*

My own proving ground to answer the eternal proposition was the South. The Atlanta bureau of CBS was my school, my confirmation. If I were to amount to anything, this is where it would happen. If I were to confront the source of all evil, what better battlefield?

The bureau responsibility extended from West Virginia in the north to the tip of Argentina in the south. Myriad stories and newsmakers awaited me, wowed me beyond description.

I was intimidated greatly by the forceful personalities I tried to capture on camera at every opportunity and during every person-to-person interview I did with them: Martin Luther King for civil rights, George Wallace for racism, Congressman John Lewis for courage, Fidel Castro for revolution and Elvis Presley for originality. Eudora Welty for her prose of unsurpassed beauty, Pat Conroy for his *Lords of Discipline* and *Prince of Tides,* Jimmy Carter for his political genius and Georgia Governor Lester Maddox for his sincere ignorance and conscientious stupidity.

No story was my favorite, no personality my darling. Each was paramount in its own way. Lessons learned from each meeting would serve me well. But perhaps those whose stories provoked me the most were ordinary people. Their local triumphs and defeats became fodder for my most compelling offerings.

Charles Kuralt gave me the chance to express their stories on his matchless *Sunday Morning* broadcast on CBS. Among my most loved—a piece recounting the suffering of poor black people in Atlanta whose children had been snatched and killed. The story aired on Easter Sunday morning, April 19, 1981, and was produced by my close friend and television genius, James Houtrides.

The story transcript is given in abbreviated form here. Visuals included church choirs singing and mourners at funerals.

> Kuralt: It's Easter. It is Passover. The day symbolizes suffering and deliverance. From Atlanta, Ed Rabel reports our Sunday Morning cover story. ...
>
> Rabel: Atlanta, like the Biblical city, is desolate. It is preoccupied with its dead, and the irony of Easter is not lost on its people. ...Atlanta has turned inward on itself. Everything is affected by the murders of black children. It never stops. ... In the beginning, Atlanta paid no attention. The first killing was in July of 1979, and the police did not know who had done it. They still do not know. But the murders continued. The police don't know who did this either. ... Now the city can hardly talk about anything else. It never stops.

Atlanta, Georgia, Mayor Maynard Jackson: Yes, this dominates the skyline; it dominates the tapestry of … of our lives. It has to be the major concern. If it were not that way, we would not be a responsible city.

Rabel: The city dwells on its problem, anxious and diverted. Maynard Jackson is the first black mayor of Atlanta. He is stepping down after eight years, but his record is overshadowed, because someone is killing black children. It never stops.

Jackson (at funeral): We have no choice but to be together, because the alternative to being together is being apart. We have no choice but to love, because the alternative to loving is hating.

Rabel: Even if the city wanted to forget, it could not. There are constant reminders. Parents of the dead children remind the city that in two years there have been 23 known young black victims, two missing, and no arrests. Yusef Bell was one of those killed. His mother, Camille, will not let the city forget.

Camille Bell: Because I'm not going to be satisfied, until the cases are solved. So no matter what, you know, no matter what else goes down and no more … matter how many smoke screens are thrown up, ah-m, or whatever else is going on, it doesn't bother me. I have to get ... keep getting back to the 25 kids dead and missing in Atlanta and nobody's solved the cases. ...

Rabel: Andrew Young is running for mayor of this city, which has boasted that it is too busy to hate. Now, it is re-examining whether it has remained faithful to that slogan it earned many years ago.

Young: This city is pulling together in the face of this crisis, and we are coping with this crisis. I think we can do this because of the kind of political structure we have, the kind of cooperation we've had through the years between rich and poor, and between black and white.

Rabel: Ivan Allen [who used to be mayor] is credited with leading Atlanta to success in the mid-sixties, when other Southern cities blundered into violence at the beginning of the civil rights movement.

Allen: I think there was a full realization here of the fact that there was a great crusade sweeping across America and probably the world under our democratic system for the equal rights of the people, human decency. ... They can't understand why we can't resolve it, and they look at it as ... as a great problem. And I see it and I hear it

46

every day, when I am out of Atlanta. And I just came in from New York, and I … that's all I heard. And … and we have … we've got to stick together, until all our forces, together with Atlanta people, get a resolution to it. …

Rabel: Suddenly, amidst this glittering hub of communications and business, some things overlooked in the past are becoming more visible. Nearly a quarter of the population is poverty stricken. All of the murder victims have come from these poor neighborhoods.

Young: It's also forcing us to look at the differences within rich and poor Atlanta and ask questions about the lifestyles of our children, particularly in single-parent homes, or in … in … the sort of latch-key children, where both parents happen to be working and where children are free—in the streets until five-thirty, six o'clock at night. It's made us look at the problem of youth instead of just taking it for granted.

Rabel: The reappraisal goes on. It is fostered by the agony of parents of dead youngsters enduring the spectacle of defending themselves in the street over suggestions by the FBI that some parents are responsible for some of the deaths.

Rabel to Mrs. Bell: Did you ever take a lie detector test?

47

Bell: All of us, most of us have taken lie-detector tests with the police department. The FBI says that someone within my family is suspect. That's what they said. That's only reason I feel that way, that's the only reason I find it necessary to answer that.

Venus Taylor, mother of a victim: How in the hell could I do a horrible thing like that to my own child? ...

Rabel: The killings threaten to become the overriding issue in the mayoral campaign now underway. The candidates have tacitly agreed to avoid the subject, but it is unavoidable as the people search for answers. And candidate Reginald Eaves, a former police commissioner, says he won't refuse to answer *the* question.

Rabel to Eaves: ... If you were mayor or had access to doing something more about that, what methods and what way would you go about dealing with that?

Eaves: The commitment that I have is that I have always had the kind of government where you can touch me, and I can touch you. And I am convinced that, by my moving through the community as often as I ... as I did in the ward, and raising the kind of questions with the kind of people who

48

will have the knowledge, that just like I saw, that at least 10 homicides in two years where we didn't have one iota of evidence, we will be able to do the same thing in this kind of setting.

Rabel to Young: You don't want to talk about it. Why is that?

Young: Because the only thing you can do is put the police on trial and that's not our objective. Our objective is to put the killers on trial. And we feel as though the police are doing everything they possibly can toward that end.

Jackson: The threats … to all the wonderful things about Atlanta, the threat is always there. And the longer this persists, the more acute the threat becomes, but we have suffered intense feelings before, nothing quite like this, nothing as horrible as this, nothing as heart-rending as this. But what we're going to do is to do whatever we have to do as long as we have to do it. …

Rabel: Atlanta is a place where parents are afraid to let their children play outside alone. The murders have done that. It never stops. But Easter brings hope in its message, and the children are outside to celebrate. …

Young: The Christian message is that God does triumph over suffering, just as from the crucifixion there did come a

resurrection which saved mankind. Out
of these tragic crucifixions of our
children, there can come a resurrection
of this city and of this nation. And,
hopefully, we should be attempting to
be sensitive to what God might be
doing in our midst in order to raise up a
new people, a people who … of faith
and a people who are concerned about
their young, and a people who are
dedicated to helping the least of these
in our society to survive and live
meaningful lives as God's children.

At the time, I voraciously consumed Andrew Young's
rightful words. All my life I devoured educated statements
and astonishing images by digesting them without letting
them go. They took root inside me and woke me up and put
me to sleep. The voices of wisdom not only whispered to
me from outside, but startled my inner-being all the time.
When my childhood Methodist minister spoke to me about
the malevolence of racism, I nodded in strong agreement,
for his words paralleled and duplicated an almost instinctive
understanding of things I already knew. Neither he nor
school opened my eyes. They were already wide open.
While all my juvenile playmates wallowed in bullyism and
racism and self-loathing, I was out there on the fringes of
the playground keeping my eye on the ball and delighting in
the universal verities I had picked up, somehow, along the
way. Maybe I was inspired. I still don't know how I was
imbued with the truth, but I am glad for it. Those absolutes
kept me out of trouble. They also made me odd. I did not fit
in.

Parental guidance was fictional. Alcoholism tore at my
father's self-worth despite his talent for artistry. Hysteria
had broken my mother in her youth when both of her

parents, the grandmother and grandfather I never met, died violently. A coal miner in West Virginia, my maternal grandfather suffered irreparable internal injuries in a mining accident. Then my maternal grandmother was injured severely while traveling back to her Illinois roots from West Virginia to bury her coal miner husband. The car in which she was a passenger went out of control and tumbled down a West Virginia mountainside. She died of cancer two years later. My mother never recovered from the emotional trauma. Neither she nor my dad was in any position to instill in me the high-mindedness I adopted egoistically. But they did give me, unwittingly and without malice, the brain I used as I saw fit. I used it effectively to personally disgorge myself from the poverty, ignorance, racism, and provincialism that claimed almost all my classmates.

The odds were against me. Right from the beginning, my fellows and I were damaged goods. Born white and male just as black and female were on the ascendancy, things didn't look good. The chances of making it out of the mountains of impoverishment—both physically and intellectually—were slim to none. Coal mining was a lost cause. Harvard was not only out-of-reach but out of my league. The avenues to the foreign service career I longed for were traveled by Yale and Princeton men, not Morris Harvey boys.

Yet, my imagination did not fail me. The blood, hot and furious, that shocked me into other-world self-awareness when I was a child at grandpa's feet, I could not wash off. It was all over me, inside me, pushing me forward incessantly. It would not let go. I went so fast to try to escape that the shackles of deprivation fell off by their own accord. The wind on my face blurred the vision of intolerance that tried to take hold. Finally, I could see clearly now the bright and shining goal. By the sheer act of imagining my destiny I achieved it. Innate consciousness of

51

and sensitivity about my own humanity and intelligence that rejected my poor background made it happen. Thus when I arrived, fully formed in a condition of renaissance on the battleground of racism in the south, I was ready to smash that evil to smithereens by exposing it with all my power and passion.

Therefore, restating here in great detail this defining moment in the life and times of Atlanta, and by extension, the South and all of America, should bring us up to date on where we stand on the question of race. To this day, there is no real closure on racism in Atlanta and America at large. Although the alleged killer was arrested and convicted, Atlanta's fear was not assuaged. Even now, the "missing and murdered children" story goes unresolved to skeptics who blame a conspiracy to get Atlanta off the racial hook.

A young black man, Wayne Williams, is serving two life sentences for the gruesome crimes that terrorized Atlanta during the three years when up to 50 black children went missing. According to many, including some parents of the victims, the conclusion was too neat. To end Atlanta's agony, they say, the FBI and white politicians and even Mayor Jackson conspired to deep-six an investigation that showed Ku Klux Klan involvement. The Klan, they believe, was on a mission to kill black children as a method of "cleansing" the city. But immediately following the arrest of Williams, the kidnappings and murders stopped. Atlanta's anguish was over. Yet questions remain. In race, in America, questions always remain. Because no matter how much we would like to believe we are too busy to hate, the vast racial divide comes back to haunt us.

9
Not a Drive-By Shooting

*For what is life? A madness. What is life? An illusion, a
shadow, a story.
And the greatest good is little enough …*
—Pedro Calderón de la Barca (17th century)

I learned other lessons while starting out in the South. A
whole new set of instructions came with the territory. Some
assembly was required. I stayed up all night trying to put it
together. Every time I turned around, the handlebars would
fall off and I would have to reconnect the whole thing.

Race permeated the setting. Every day and in every way,
black nationhood and white citizenry seemed to clash
openly and inwardly. Up North the tension over proper
positioning in every situation didn't seem to occur. But in
the South, a new set of rules governed the daily deeds so
pervasively I was on tenterhooks all the time.

Some perverse person or persons had set up the game a
long time ago and now everybody had to play it.
Sometimes there was no subtlety in the moves you had to
make. Just think of the movie *The Help* if you want pitch
perfect. Most times I just could not make it out. A blind got
in the way, the kind of blind that separates the
Mississippians and the Minnesotans.

Now I'll stop hinting at it. Sooner or later you've got to put a
limit on haziness. The best way to describe it accurately is
to recount the Hughes Rudd episode. To do so, I must
explain a little about Hughes Rudd.

When I was writing this book I contacted Peter M. Herford, who probably knew Hughes Rudd as well as anyone in the business, to make sure I got the description of the man and the incident right. Herford said Rudd was the best writer CBS News or any other news organization ever had, and Herford was happy to fill me on Rudd's younger days.

During World War II Rudd flew a Piper Cub, the kind used to spot and guide artillery fire. "That meant flying low," Herford said, remembering Hughes' words. The age of Hughes in his tale may not fit the official biography, but he told Herford he "went in as a teenager—might have been underage, but he was flying in the war at 18. The planes had tandem seating, with the spotter sitting behind the pilot." Long after Herford and Rudd started working together the older man opened up about one of his experiences. He was flying a mission and wondered why the spotter in the back seat had gone silent. He looked down and saw a brownish liquid coming from the back between his legs. The spotter was dead, shot from the bottom up. Hughes was the only one of 18 in his unit who came out alive.

Herford said Rudd was "a tortured human being to his death …shaped by his experience in World War II and never was able to excise the terror.

"Hughes meandered after the war but was a writer by passion, talent and skill. A short form writer, his novellas are well known in literary circles thanks to publication by *The Paris Review*.. . . He had an eye, an ear, and the words to bring what he saw, heard, and felt, to life."

For all of us, working with Rudd was a challenge. Herford was one of the first to discover this fact. "When I worked my first stories with him," Herford said, "I expected pearls to come out of his fingers. . . . Instead he sat and stared at his keyboard. (He did not drink until after we had filed, in my experience.) He stared, he stared. At first I panicked and nagged. He slapped me down with a look that said, *buzz off kid.* I fretted, and sweated, and made excuses for 'no script yet' to the CBS Evening News executive producer in New York. As editing deadline approached. . .my heart took on apoplectic rhythms with no ability to scream or rant."

Suddenly then, when it seemed all was lost, Herford would hear the single-finger typing. Rudd would be hugging the little Hermes typewriter with his left arm, his head hovering over the keyboard, as he typed a steady rhythm for about five minutes. The script would appear, then, described by Herford as "a jewel." He does not remember a piece by Rudd ever needing an edit or change, no matter whether it was hard news or a feature. "Gifted. Genius," Herford declared.

The drink came after the writing. All of us recognized he was an alcoholic. However, it was controlled. To the best of Herford's knowledge, this was true in Rudd's anchor days as well. After the work was done, however, he consumed stunning quantities of booze.

Remember, this is Atlanta in the 1970s—a city too busy to hate that hated nonetheless. CBS's Atlanta bureau chief, a white guy born in the Deep South who should have known better, called Rudd in New York and suggested he should hightail it down to Atlanta for a story. Only Rudd, not we unsophisticated scribes already attached to the bureau, could do the story justice. Rudd, with his cosmopolitan ways, would be perfect to provide viewers with the cynic's point of view, the point of view with which we lowly users of the escritoire could not be trusted.

So the mightily cynical CBS News Correspondent Hughes Rudd and his producer, Peter Herford, arrived at the bureau to be greeted by a flurry of handshakes and pontification. Rudd was in a rush to be taken to ground zero, the location of the story the bureau chief had so ardently touted. In those days, just beneath the surface of conviviality between the races, there persisted the time-honored stratification in which every person knew his place and stuck by it. No exceptions, even if you think you have a good story.

The story was no good. This was no time or place to be doing a thing like this. Upon closer examination, it was not something that should have been done at any time, in any place. I wasn't there when the bureau chief proudly presented Hughes with his masterpiece, and I'm glad I wasn't. Hughes was not pleased, to say the least. He was apoplectic to say the most. Hughes, you see, had just gotten a good look at the site he had been dragged all the way from New York to visit, the place *populaire* he was going to ridicule, the object of his misdirection. It was a funeral home, but not just any funeral home. A drive-in funeral home. Yes, you could drive right by and see the loved one through a plate glass window. That would be a dead person on public display for all to see, a damsel in no distress, if you will. But you won't, nor would Hughes.

There was an untold story, a little fact the bureau chief had failed to provide Rudd, and a slight oversight the Anglo-Saxon chief would regret the rest of his life. Our *chef-du-bureau*, his deep-South blinders on, never thought to tell Rudd the object of his affection was a black, drive-in funeral home. Real, dead African-Americans were putting on a show for the parade of cars and trucks—not a sight for sore eyes, especially the eyes of the nation at a time when we were trying to get over our racist habits. Rudd immediately sank into his cups.

By the time we arrived at the swanky downtown restaurant to which Rudd had invited all hands, he was plastered. This was one of those dining establishments that hang out four stars for you to see and $$$ you don't see coming. But who cared? Rudd was paying for it. This was a place in which you are surrounded by frumpy, old rich broads sporting bejeweled glasses and bouffant hairdos. Remember, this was the '70s.You could have cut the syrupy southern drawls with a butter knife.

All hands had seated themselves near Rudd—the red-faced chief, his wife, my wife and I, the other hands and their wives. Several double scotches and some really good wine had transformed Rudd the cynic into Rudd the apostate out to do us all in. He zeroed in on me and the better half.

"Hey, Ed, how did you meet your wife?"

"No, Hughes," I responded, warning him off. "You really don't want to hear that story. It is rather corny, after all." But he insisted.

"Aw, come on," Rudd slurred. "Let us hear it."

"Well, okay, if you insist. We met in high school. We were childhood sweethearts. It was fate," I muttered quietly.

"In high school?" Rudd railed, his voice soaring into the rafters for all to hear. "In high school," he shouted. "You know something, Rabel?" (It was an E.F. Hutton moment.) "That's about as interesting as a pack of wild dogs rolling over in their own shit." And Hughes wasn't just whistlin' Dixie.

10
Mendacity

We know how to speak falsehoods which resemble real things,
but we know, when we will, how to speak true things.
—Hesiod (c 700 b.c.)

Racism in my workplace wasn't the only thing that bewildered me. Outright mendacity was commonplace. The more I learned about the business I was in, the more I wondered about it. This was something I had wanted with all my heart and soul since I was 15 years of age. I had covered the entire battlefield with a smoke screen, and now I was in the clear, out of the fog and into the bright light of reality.

During the period between 1973 and the early 1980s, I often covered events in Central America. On one of those occasions, when Geraldo Rivera and his camera crew were outside the U.S. Embassy, I saw him encourage a protester to throw red paint on the embassy walls so his camera crew could film the anti-American scene. Geraldo's perjury was becoming his brand.

I wasn't really surprised. Around 1967-68, I had been part of a similar setup. I went to a residence with a CBS producer who said the topic of our interview was junk mail. On our way to the home, he explained further that the alleged victim had not really received an overload of mail. But, he said, she was going to say, on camera, that she was overwhelmed with letters and magazines and other pieces of unwanted postings. And she would be telling a falsehood, of course.

Countless times I saw network camera people filming scenes they had orchestrated. Usually the camera had failed to catch the scene in its original form. A repeat of the scene was bogus. But it was the scene the TV news audience would see. And how taken in they would be.

If anyone should not be lying, it is the messenger. But it happens all the time. Networks produce standards guidebooks that reporters, producers and camera people are instructed to follow on penalty of dismissal if they fail to do so. However, the guidelines are frequently ignored. Offenders argue their offenses are trivial, not to be confused with high news crimes like the infamous "Waiting to Explode" episode of November 17, 1992, on *Dateline NBC.*

The *60 Minutes* style program was about General Motors pickups allegedly exploding upon impact during accidents due to the poor design of fuel tanks. *Dateline*'s film showed a sample of a low speed accident with the fuel tank exploding. In reality, *Dateline NBC* producers had caused the truck's fuel tank to be rigged with remotely controlled explosives. The program did not disclose the fact that the accident was staged. GM investigators studied the film and discovered smoke actually came out of the fuel tank six frames *before* impact. GM subsequently filed an anti-defamation/libel lawsuit against NBC after conducting an extensive investigation. On Monday, February 8, 1993, after announcing the lawsuit, GM conducted a highly publicized point-by-point rebuttal in the Product Exhibit Hall of the General Motors Building in Detroit that lasted nearly two hours. The lawsuit was settled the same week by NBC, and anchor Jane Pauley read a 3-minute, 30-second on-air apology to viewers.

The lawsuit and subsequent settlement were arguably the most devastating blows for NBC in a series of reputation-damaging incidents during the 1990s and early 2000s. Within NBC, Michael Gartner, who resigned shortly after the incident, was the source for much of the blame. In 1988, NBC News President Reuven Frank had hired Gartner to be the NBC News top officer, despite his having no TV news background. This was an attempt to satisfy parent-company General Electric by replacing current journalists with cheaper, less experienced reporters and producers.

In addition to Gartner's forced resignation, three *Dateline NBC* producers were dismissed: Jeff Diamond, executive producer; David Rummel, senior producer, and Robert Read, producer of the report on the pickups. Michele Gillen, the reporter involved in the segment, was transferred to Miami station WTVJ.

You would think after that train wreck, double-dealing TV audiences would be a thing of the past. And you would be wrong. I did turn in my producer on that phony junk mail story. It was the right thing to do. He was given only a slap on the wrist. Somehow I was made out to be the culprit by my bosses for incriminating my cohort. Lesson learned.

11
Jimmy Carter in Margaritaville

*If we could just have a government
that is as good and honest and decent and pure
and as filled with love, as are the American people,
what a wonderful government we would have.*
—Jimmy Carter

Jimmy Carter is a son of the South. A former governor of Georgia, he decided to run for the presidency after Richard Nixon resigned in humiliation over Watergate. Carter was perfect for the job. An outsider, he was the reverse of the inside-the-beltway crowd. America had had it with the insiders in Washington. Americans longed for a fresh, decent voice in the oval office. Carter suited the requirement. The biggest problem was almost nobody outside Georgia knew him or knew of him. On the campaign trail, the former Georgia governor would pass through a crowd of voters, shaking their hands and radiating that perpetual Eleanor Roosevelt smile. As he passed by, most of those whom he had greeted would look to each other in bewilderment. "Who was that?" they'd ask.

After my bosses at CBS assigned correspondents to cover the field of candidates running for the presidency in the primaries, they realized they had failed to designate a reporter who would cover Carter. That's what an afterthought he was. My superiors in New York cast their eyes toward the Atlanta bureau for a correspondent they could attach to Carter, and decided I would do just fine. They thought it would be a short assignment. "Carter isn't going anywhere," they said as they snorted. Months into the primary season, seven days a week, 24 hours a day, I was still on the heels of Jimmy Carter. He had shocked his opponents, winning handily to become the Democratic nominee. Nobody was more amazed than I.

We were engaging in repartee one night in an Atlanta bar— Sam Donaldson, Judy Woodruff and I. Nothing witty, sort of chitchat. Carter, the next President of the United States? That was the question. Donaldson, known for wearing the worst toupee in television history, was covering the Carter campaign for ABC. Woodruff, the excellent broadcast journalist who has covered politics and other news for more than three decades for CNN, NBC and National Public Television, was NBC's star on the campaign.

On any national campaign for the presidency there is the campaign and then there is the campaign subtext. A lot goes on behind the scenes you never hear about. Important stuff, scandalous stuff, criminal stuff, *Behind the Green Door* stuff (for those of you who remember the '60s), and Bill Clinton stuff (for those of you who, oh never mind). The things you never hear about are the things reporters never want you to hear about because they, the reporters, are the culprits. You talk about your cover-ups. (Or is it covers-up?) Anyway, here's what happened in that bar.

We were prattling along about this and that happening somewhere on the campaign bus, fear and loathing, the latest gossip about one campaign worker or the other, who was sleeping with whom, how soon we thought Carter would realize he had no chance, you know, really important chatter.

Judy announced she was going to the little girl's room. The gentlemen we were, Sam and I stood up to let the lady pass. *Wham!* Out of nowhere, Sam grabs Judy's arm and sinks his teeth into her wrist. I mean Sam actually bit Judy on the wrist. I had heard Sam was known to bite women on the ass, but here he was, in front of God and everybody, biting this nice lady. Judy screamed a little bit. I turned red, the straight arrow that I was, my cheeks burning at the improbable sight. Judy sat down and ordered another drink. What prompted this bushy eye-browed, toupee wearing, middle aged scribe on the far side of forty to take a hunk out of Judy's wrist? Lord, he could have maimed her for life. And he was married. I guess you just have to sum it up to Sam being Sam. He was one of the most entertaining of all the people I have met. Not the stern gatecrasher out to rain on every parade he could find. This interloper with the eyes of the devil was human, really human. And poor back then.

On the campaign bus Sam was vexed and in need. He wanted the bus to stop and let him off. Something had to be fixed. What is it, Sam? What's wrong? Sam pulled up the cuff of his trousers and pointed to his shoe. "Look," he said, "holes." Sam had holes in the bottom of his shoes. Not just scuff marks. The holes went right through to his socks. "Get me to a cobbler," he pleaded. Today the man is a millionaire. Go figure.

12
Act of Desperation

It is a characteristic of wisdom not to do desperate things.
--Henry David Thoreau

The late Hamilton Jordan was Carter's brilliant campaign strategist. He wrote the 76-page treatise for Carter on how to win the presidency. One evening after Carter got the nomination, I unwisely told Jordan how surprised I was with Carter's win. Jordan turned to me and said, "Not half as surprised as we are that a junior correspondent like you was assigned to cover my boss." *Touché.*

Carter's victory was an awakening to just how desperately a lot of Americans yearned for someone who would tell the truth. In his campaign speeches, Carter pounded away on his primary thesis: "I promise I will never lie to you," he repeated over and over again. Never mind where he stood on the issues of the day. Democrats knew that after years of deception and dissembling by Nixon they had a winner, or so they thought.
Carter almost lost it to Gerald Ford in the general election. He blew a 33-point lead, in part because voters had started not to trust this newcomer. The late Jody Powell, Carter's remarkable press secretary, told me later Carter feared he would lose the election because of the key question I asked the future president. The lack of trust started with that inquiry.

I wanted to know why he had used the words "ethnic purity" to describe, in a newspaper interview, his position on whether housing in the suburbs should be purposely integrated. The newspaper reporter had quoted Carter as saying if he became president he would like to maintain the "ethnic purity" of some neighborhoods. CBS News and I picked up the troubling quote, even though it was buried in the 24th paragraph of the article. Carter's comeback to my questioning instantly became front page news.

Pressed to explain, Carter's face reddened with anger and he began to sweat. Instead of softening his language, he spoke of housing policies in terms of "black intrusion," of "alien groups," and of a "diametrically opposite kind of family." Many of his opponents charged Carter with searching for votes among the white ethnic urban Democratic voters hostile to government housing programs that brought racial integration.

His main supporters were livid. Slamming his fist against his desk, Atlanta's Mayor Maynard Jackson postponed plans to endorse Carter and angrily exclaimed, "Is there no white politician I can trust?"

Mayor Richard Hatcher of Gary, Indiana, declared: "We've created a Frankenstein monster with a Southern drawl, a more cultured version of the old Confederate at the schoolhouse door."

"He is only giving ammunition to those who would divide America," added civil rights activist Bayard Rustin of New York.

Jesse Jackson, then director of Chicago's Operation PUSH, called Carter's views "a throwback to Hitlerian racism."

The terminology "ethnic purity" certainly sounded like Hitler to me. Was the usage intentional? Or was Carter clueless? Although he was alive during World War II, served in the U.S. Navy as an officer under Admiral Hyman Rickover (father of the nuclear Navy) and was a progressive governor at the height of the Civil Rights movement, Carter, somehow, seemed not to understand how Nazi-like he continued to sound.

The angst, of course, was more than in Carter's position on integrating housing; the problem was in his use of bizarre language. If Martin Luther King's father had not come to Carter's rescue, he most certainly would have lost the election to Gerald Ford. Carter apologized for his near fatal gaffe. And King Sr. embraced Carter in a public ceremony on Peachtree Street in downtown Atlanta, helping restore blacks to the fold and Carter's credibility as a possible winner.

Democrats went on to elect him, "giving us," some Republicans say, "possibly the worst president of the 20th century."

After Carter won the nomination, newspapers and news divisions assigned top notch reporters and correspondents to identify the Georgia phenomenon. One of them was the distinguished scribe Jim Wooten of *The New York Times.* Jim and I were fast friends, following Carter everywhere. On the press plane flying from California to Ohio, we broke out the tequila and salt and other ingredients he bought in bulk before takeoff. The trip would, forevermore, be known as the infamous "Margarita Flight." This was back when reporters were known to drink like fish. We had no time for adopting present day behavior elicited by preppy journalists drinking bottled water and doing pre-dawn runs. Heavy drinking was the norm for us. Reporters on that flight got really drunk.

After we had knocked back several glasses of the tequila drink, Jim and I decided to record on audio tape, a mock interview with Governor Averell Harriman, the great defender of the Democratic Party. It seemed like the right thing to do at the time. Jim wrote the script. This is the same Wooten who topped his Arizona "pool" report for us reporters with this sentence: "Arizona sunrises, like little gypsy girls, do magic to the soul of man."

I portrayed Walter Cronkite and Averell Harriman. Jim played himself. This is how I remember the interview.

> Walter Cronkite: Good evening. This is Walter Cronkite. Tonight we have an exclusive interview with Governor Averell Harriman, the scion of the Democratic Party. Harriman has endorsed Governor Jimmy Carter for president. He is traveling with Carter tonight aboard a plane from California to Ohio. James Wooten, reporter for *The New York Times* caught up with Harriman on the flight. Here is his report.

> Jim Wooten: Governor, how is it to back Carter as the standard-bearer for the political party you love so much?

> Averell Harriman: Well Jim, between you and me, it's a bitch. This is the party of Franklin Roosevelt, Harry Truman and Jack Kennedy. Quite frankly, I'll never understand how this Georgia upstart got the nomination.

> Wooten: But governor, you have shouted his praises all over the place. Indeed you are traveling with him, standing beside him on campaign stops. You will be supporting him when we land in Ohio tonight, won't you?

67

Harriman: Ohio? Ohio? Are you sure? That
little son-of-a-bitch lied to me. Carter
lied to me, told me we were going to
New York. I was so looking forward to
seeing my wife Pammy in New York,
prissy little bitch. I was gonna get me
some. That snot-nosed little bastard
from backwater Georgia has betrayed
me. He pretends to lead the
Democratic Party. I'll never accept that!
It is *my* party, my daddy bought it for
me!

We played the taped interview for Powell, Carter's aide on
the plane. His uproarious laughter must have reached to
the front of the aircraft where Carter sat. Carter demanded
to hear the tape, too. When the imitations of Cronkite and
Harriman hit him, Carter doubled up in amusement,
guffawing and pounding on the table before him.

Years later when I meet my fellow reporters from the
"Margarita Flight," invariably the first thing for which I am
remembered by them is that Harriman tape. Never mind
"ethnic purity" or my laborious effort to get the campaign
right editorially. If I go down in history for anything, it will be
that moment on the plane when we made fun of ourselves.
Glory be!

13
An Admirable Colleague

The reward of a thing well done, is to have done it.
—Ralph Waldo Emerson

My good friend and colleague Ed Bradley was my teammate at CBS News covering President Carter's campaign. Bradley died of leukemia in November 2006. He was a pioneering black journalist who was a fixture in American living rooms on Sunday nights for more than a quarter of a century on *60 Minutes*. Bradley got along with Carter about as well as I did—not well. Ed and I tag-teamed one another by watching Carter and his campaign tenaciously. That meant the artery in Carter's temple throbbed violently nearly every time he saw one of our reports. You always knew when Carter was upset because of his thumping blood vessels.

I never meant to upset Carter. Nor did Ed have it in for the former president. Yet when Ed asked Carter what he thought about a story he had done for Cronkite's show, Carter replied, "I thought it was crummy." We were doing our job. I was not an attack dog, nor a lap dog. I was a watch dog, on alert for inconsistencies, lies, prevarications, and all the other slight-of-hand paraphernalia adorning every campaign, all campaigners, and all parties.

Ed was from the rough and tumble neighborhoods of Philadelphia. I am white bread from Charleston, West Virginia. It was, therefore, with some merriment that he and I were the targets of misidentification. Standing side-by-side on the campaign trail, folks would approach the bearded Bradley to compliment him saying: "Say, you're Ed

Rabel aren't you? I love your reporting," they would say. "Keep up the good work, Rabel."

Finally one day, Ed responded to an admirer exclaiming, "You've got to understand something. There's a big difference between me and Rabel. I'm the one with the beard."

I bow to no one in my admiration for Ed as an unwavering friend and for his professionalism. He was among the very best reporters assigned to Carter. He outdid me as a chronicler, winning 19 Emmy Awards during his long career at CBS. Both Ed and I put in extended hours of sweat and toil to make sure the TV audiences we were talking to heard and saw the truth. We kept nothing from one another as we navigated the political mine fields out on the trail. If anyone deserved to be promoted to the Carter White House beat, it was Ed Bradley.

I was damaged goods, a white man on whose shift everything bad had happened. We white males were to blame for the defeat in Vietnam. We were guilty of beating black people to a pulp in their struggle for civil rights. We had dominated women for thousands of years. We were jerks in denial. Our time was over.

Carter was among the first presidents to open up opportunities in the federal government on a grand scale to women and blacks. His appointments were hailed by civil rights leaders he had courted during his campaign. Women were especially prized. He counted his wife, Rosalyn (pronounced Rose-Ah-Lin), as a top advisor. He was a progressive southern governor. But he was much more than that. He did the right thing at the right time.

CBS, in particular, had come under intense criticism for failing to put blacks in positions of importance in both its entertainment and news divisions. Most entertainers were

white. So were most reporters/correspondents. Jesse Jackson was central in the criticism that stung Bill Paley and his Tiffany Network. Change had to come.
Ed Bradley was rightly elevated to the coveted position as White House reporter. That Ed earned the promotion was never in doubt. Still, when asked why Rabel had been passed over for a White House spot, John Lane, producer for Cronkite, bluntly responded that it was a "black thing." Ed Bradley got the job, he said, "because Bradley is black."

Not so.

14
We Shall *Not* Overcome

Our Constitution is color-blind, and neither knows nor tolerates
classes among citizens. In respect of civil rights, all citizens are equal before the law.
The humblest is the peer of the most powerful.
—John Marshall Harlan, Dissenting opinion, *Plesy v. Ferguson*, 1896

Jimmy Carter, Hughes Rudd, George Wallace, Lester Maddox, James Earl Ray, MLK Jr., Andy Young and Jesse Jackson were just a few of the historical figures responsible for personally embossing my psyche regarding the unsolved problem of racism in my time. President Barack Obama, The Rev. Al Sharpton, former Secretary of State Condoleezza Rice and Associate Justice of the Supreme Court Clarence Thomas are just a few of the historical figures responsible for imprinting on contemporary souls the unsolved problem of racism in this time.

If the years of witness to unspeakable acts of racism in America have taught me anything, it is this: *There is no such thing as a post-racial America.*

Deeply ingrained in the American legend is the unmitigated fact of slavery that has burdened the country and its people since the nation was founded. As much as Americans would like to think in the 21st century they are over the high crimes and creepy deceptions caused by the travesties of racial discrimination, they are simply in deep denial.

America is still bound up in early bigotry and narrow-mindedness that threaten the national prospect. Issues about lackluster economy and poverty and homelessness pale in comparison to the dangers latent racism pose. The possibility of another war in the Middle East comes nowhere close to the risks *Pax Americana* must confront in not facing up to its disreputable racial background.

The paradigm for the self-defeating racial malignancy can be seen vividly in the laundry list of racial insults hurled at President Obama from prominent figures who've called him "uppity," a "tar baby," and "boy." Opposition to Mr. Obama comes, in most cases, not for his policies, ideas and legislation but because of *him*, who he is, America's first black president.

At the bottom of America's intransigence over race lies the indisputable failure by the media—and Americans in general—to talk and debate openly the subject of race and to put racial incidents in a historical context.

Talking openly about race is something I have tried to do throughout my professional life. On July 17, 1983, Diane Sawyer introduced my *"Indianola, Mississippi"* story on *CBS Sunday Morning*. Jesse Lee, a white matron of the South and white patron of southern ways, had invited her black maid, Rebecca Hawkins, to attend a special party at her house not as a servant, but as a guest. Such an invitation in Mississippi at that time was unheard of, a tongue-wagger *in extremis*.

Return with me now to those thrilling days of yesteryear—days that looked uncommonly like the days of today.

The transcript for that program included footage showing still shots of the unprecedented garden party with blacks

73

and whites mingling socially together. Here is the transcript in abbreviated form:

> Diane Sawyer: Something happened in Indianola, Mississippi, the other day. *The New York Times* thought it was so important that it put it on page one. And what was the news? That black people and white people went to a garden party together. That is news, in Indianola. But did it really make much difference in people's lives? That's the question in our cover story, reported this morning by Ed Rabel.

> Ed Rabel: It was a quiet Sunday in Indianola, Mississippi. Nothing much happened. People went to church, blacks and whites, separate as usual. … Black church, white church; the message is the same. Yet, in Indianola, deep in the Mississippi Delta, there is a wariness between the races. Blacks and whites live on opposite sides of the railroad tracks, but they are separated by more than that—by the memory that Indianola in the 1950s was the birthplace of the segregationist White Citizens Council; by the memory of the racial strife that erupted in the 1960s when blacks sought the right to vote; by the knowledge that until this day there is still only token integration in Indianola's public schools; and by the knowledge that the city's only public swimming pool is used by blacks only. … It may not seem like much for a

black man to come home to, but this is the irony. B.B. King, who was born in Indianola, has been coming back here every year for the last four years, to touch his past, to see his family, to play his music. ... He is America's most famous blues singer, and Indianola has admired him, gloried in his success, but never told him so in quite the same way as it did this year. In a special celebration, the city named a two-lane street B.B. King Road.

King: I don't think the Prodigal Son got the blessings that I got when I came in. That's a great feeling.

Rabel: But the most remarkable part of the celebration happened here in this private garden in Indianola, where some of the town's most prominent citizens threw a party for B.B. King. They invited 125 leading white citizens and an equal number of blacks, and the guests mingled and drank together. It was the first time ever anything like that happened in Indianola. ... It was a very private party. The snapshots were taken by one of the hostesses. The press was excluded. It was an experiment Indianola was not sure would work.

Party Hostess Jessie Lee: You know, any time you're going to have a party around here in Indianola, then

Rebecca is the one you call, 'cause she's always there in an emergency.

Rabel: Jesse Lee was one of the sponsors of the party. As in the past, she called on Rebecca Hawkins to help out. Only this time, there was a difference.

Lee: So, I called Rebecca and asked her, would she please make us 50 dozen little biscuits. And I said, "Rebecca, I just want you to know this, you are going to get an invitation to the party, and this is one time you will not have to serve yourself. You will be served." And she said, "Glory be!"

Rebecca Hawkins: When she first called me, I thought she meant to make food for the party, as I always have done. And when she said, "Come dressed and be served," then that was sort of a shock. But it was a pleasant one.

Jim Abbott, a party host and publisher of Indianola's weekly newspaper: I think that I would be less than candid if I didn't tell you that there was a ... a little trepidation among the hosts, going into the party and inviting people to come to such a party. ... I think that it ... it probably couldn't have taken place in 1963 for certain, for certain, and possibly not even in 1973. It could probably ... in '63, there would have been an incident here in the community if ... if such an integrated

76

party had taken place, I think. But we've come a long ways, and we've come light years from 1963.

Rabel: There is another measure of distance they've traveled in Indianola. Look who was invited to the party. ... Jack Harper, the county's chief administrative officer and a one-time member of the White Citizens Council; and John Chance, assistant principal at Indianola Junior High.

John Chance: And I guess wherever there's more than one race, there are problems, but the ... the thing is once the problem is identified, and I guess there is no calamity in having racial problems, the real calamity is not doing very much about it.

Jack Harper: I really think that the activity was good for the community. I think it validated and documented good will. I think it's an activity that'll serve as a springboard for other visible acceptable efforts of creating good will.

Chance: But I never believed I would see a gathering like that, and to me that said something that maybe this is the beginning of racial harmony in Indianola. It has to start somewhere.

Charles McLaurin, [who did not go], president of the local NAACP: Overall, I would say that it ... it was a fluke. It was a

77

front. It was a way of trying to make something seem good, when, in fact, it's bad. I don't see much … much progress that's going to come out of that, in terms of political and economic development. I don't … I wouldn't know that at this point any of those whites who were involved in that party are going to be inviting blacks back to any other parties, unless B.B. King comes back again.

Rabel to Jesse Lee: Tell me something. Why is it that blacks and whites in Indianola do not socialize more as they did the other day when you brought them together at this party for B.B. King?

Lee: Well, our past—I mean—all right, Rebecca has her friends, her group of friends. We're friends, yes. She doesn't want to come over here and have dinner with me, do you?

Hawkins: No. (Laughing) No. I have too many … too many affairs of my own.

Lee: That's exactly right.

Rabel: Weeks after the party, there was a political rally in an empty lot in the black section of town. As usual, the politicians showed up looking for votes. … Blacks and whites come together in Indianola for politics or business, but they do not mingle socially. … Yet something happened in Indianola. The party for B.B. King won't go away. It has taken on a life of its own, a meaning of its own.

Rabel: Something happened in Indianola.

Chance: Maybe this is the beginning of racial harmony in Indianola. It has to start somewhere.

McLaurin: It was a fluke. It was a front. It was a way of trying to make something seem good, when in fact it's bad.

Lee: I think it's a matter of … kind of being able to talk to each other. But I mean, we've listened to each other's problems, and just like Rebecca, when my child was killed, walked in that side door and there was Rebecca. When her husband was killed, I was down there, too. And, you know, when you have mourned with each other, I mean, we've also been happy with each other, too.

Hawkins: Oh, yes.

Lee: We surely have, Rebecca. So, I mean, we're just friends.

In the three decades since I reported that story, not much has changed in Indianola. Whites and blacks still live separately, go to separate churches and don't really mingle socially. It is self-imposed segregation, as usual. Charles McLaurin had wisdom way beyond his years.

In America in the past three decades, not much has been learned on the racial front, either. Americans point with pride to advances made in tearing down racial barriers. But when it comes to the vital stuff of respect, America still has a long way to go.

The country needs to speed up the battle against inequality and prejudice. When political campaigners are able to energize voters by denouncing and threatening Hispanics over illegal immigration, there is terrible trouble. When furious cheers arise from frustrated whites when a candidate for high office invokes the idea of electrocuting human beings if they try to scale border fences, America's ideal is adrift. When black unemployment outpaces white joblessness by a wide margin, there is tribulation brewing. And when one percent of the population controls 25 percent of the nation's wealth, that is grounds for revolution.

> *For what shall it profit a man, if he shall gain the whole world,*
> *and lose his own soul?*
> —Mark 8:36

To paraphrase the words of that warrior for justice, Martin Luther King, what does it mean to a community to know that three out of ten African-American boys growing up will spend time in prison? What does it do to the fabric of the family and community to have such a substantial proportion of its young men enmeshed in the criminal justice system? What images and values are communicated to young people who see the prisoner as the most prominent pervasive role model in the community?

The solution may be intrinsic in the manner in which America's population is growing. Estimates of the United States population at the middle of the 21st century project a nation of 400 million, or roughly 100 million more than live here now. Projections show an astonishing diversity and youthfulness at 2050.

Whites will no longer be in the majority. The U.S. minority population, currently 30 percent, is expected to exceed 50 percent before 2050.No other advanced, populous country will see such diversity. If the dominance by America's white population since the founding in 1776 has been the inscrutable genesis of the problems of racism and economic inequality, then time will take its toll on the white managers. Tea Party pathogenesis will be a thing of the past. The calculating ultra conservative wing of the Republican Party that holds its political organization hostage can simply say bye-bye. Outlandish sermonizing by old white men in pursuit of the presidency in 2012 will be seen as merely the death rattles of a lost cause in 2050.

The billions of dollars in the hands of a few today will certainly be redistributed to the many by 2050. And the loss of Anglo-Saxon control will have a beneficial impact on American democracy, not the doomsday scenario preached by those who harbor their riches and rail against the Occupy Wall Street movement.

So to all those folks who rule Americana and crush minorities today, enjoy it while you can, for your day is over.

My maternal grandmother, Mary Adele Bradley Metz, who died of cancer in 1930. Two years earlier she was injured going to Illinois from West Virginia to bury my maternal grandfather, William Metz, when her car tumbled over a West Virginia mountainside. William was a coal miner who died from injuries suffered in a West Virginia coal mine accident.

My mother, Gertrude Metz Rabel, never fully recovered from her parents' deaths that occurred when she was but a teenager.

My father, Ed, Sr., flew the West Virginia skies in a WW II-era bi-plane. He was an artist too.

I grew up a poor boy near my roots on Rabel Mountain not far from Charleston, West Virginia.

L-R Standing- Ed Rabel, Sr. (my father) Me (the skinny kid) Hubert Rabel (a cousin) Harry Rabel, Joe Sargent (a friend) John Reynolds (a friend) Douglas Rabel (brother) Seated: center- my grandfather Harry Rabel (slayer of chickens), and Charles Rabel (a cousin) holding a trout. When I was 10 years old, My father, Ed, Sr. took me on a trout fishing trip to Hunter's Run in Nicholas County, West Virginia. Cousin Hubert, friend, Joe Sargent, another friend, John Reynolds and my brother Douglas all caught fish. I caught a cold.

At age 17 I was a lad hoping for the best but knowing West Virginia was not a great spring-board.

I read the news on radio from the AP wire and dreamed of becoming a network television foreign correspondent. My dream came true just a few years later.

Rabel Rouser "committing suicide" with Gillette Blue Blades.

My escape pod from West Virginia was WCHS-TV where, as news director, I interviewed Miss Universe in 1963.

On a more serious note, I visited Washington, D.C. in 1962 to film Bobby Kennedy for my news show and, myself, to be photographed standing beside Kennedy and U.S. Senator Robert C. Byrd (D-WV) and Senator Jennings Randolph (D-WV).

CBS News was my destination. The CBS icon, the Eye, was my launching pad. WCHS-TV was a CBS affiliate.

A farewell to me by West Virginia dignitaries at WCHS-TV. I was on my
way to the big time.

In 1966 CBS News hired me as a reporter, fully registered, passport in
hand, to report wars and rumors of wars.

I covered the racial wars first. I encountered racism in Atlanta while interviewing Georgia Governor Lester "Ax Handle" Maddox. Laurens Pierce was my cameraman. Pierce, alone, took the famous, exclusive video of Gov. George Wallace being gunned down in a parking lot.

Ed Rabel and other network reporters interview Charles Evers, brother of slain civil rights leader Medgar Evers.

III
Lessons for Journalists

15
Forgetting History

A country without a memory is a country of madmen.
—George Santayana

Our current obsession with joblessness and poverty and hopelessness preoccupies the minds of the many born after the Civil Rights Movement, Vietnam and even 9/11. They cannot or choose not to relate to the brutal events their forebears experienced. Being out of work and out of a home dazzles them with the idea that the problems are brand new. They claim poverty and hunger are newfangled phenomena that require suffering as no one else has suffered.

Yet the suffering over race and, particularly, over wars and rumors of wars, has been with us a very long time. Eras of self-doubt have stymied us long before many readers of this book were born. Ten thousand Americans died in three days of bloody battle at Gettysburg even before your great-grandfathers came on the scene. Memorial days have come and gone, marching dutifully into history without your ever taking notice. So do not feel special.

One of the very few promises made by old age is that of long memory, if you are lucky. An ability to recount life's mistakes and not repeat them is good fortune, if in the recollection there is recognition that a person's past is prologue. Perhaps the "most unkindest cut of all" is a young person's rejection of prologue as trivia, not to be confused with the authentic distress of modern times.

To lay out the past vibrantly—the history of warfare, specifically—is to promote the hope the greenhorns will learn something and in so doing spare themselves the anguish of what went before. One can only hope.

On May 31, 1981, I was about the business of remembering, just as I am today. My wish then is my optimism today: simple words will be the avenue to understanding and encouragement. To do that, the viewer, the reader, must play along with me in my search for the comprehension that you are not the only ones who have suffered the slings and arrows of outrageous fortune. (Apologies to the Bard.)

It is *Sunday Morning* on CBS and here again is Charles Kuralt. The footage included action at the cemetery in Gettysburg, Pennsylvania; close-ups of tombstones with names and numbers there; scenes showing the cemeteries in Chateau-Thierry and Normandy; Vietnam veterans voicing their experiences and footage from the Vietnam War. Below is a shortened transcript:

> Kuralt: Memorial Day is not a day to glorify war. It is a day to remember the war dead—who they were, and who we are—our cover story, reported by Ed Rabel.

> Ed Rabel: Ten thousand Americans died here [in Gettysburg] in the bloodiest three-day battle in America's history. It was Gettysburg. And the dead on both sides of the Civil War were Americans.
> …

> Voice over: This is Gettysburg. But let it stand for anyplace in America and overseas

where Americans are buried. ...At
Chateau-Thierry, where American
dead of World War I are buried...all
good American names. ... And at
Omaha Beach in Normandy, where
American dead of World War II are
buried ... all good American names. ...

Rabel: All week long, Americans
remembered. President Ronald
Reagan remembered at West Point,
when he spoke to the graduating class
of 1981.

Reagan: Let friend and foe alike be made
aware of the spirit that is sweeping
across our land, because it means we
will meet our responsibility to the free
world. Very much a part of this new
spirit is patriotism, and with that goes a
heartfelt appreciation for the sacrifices
of those in uniform.

Vietnam veteran George Otto: I think there's
still feelings of ... of bitterness,
because I ... I just don't feel that the
people who made sacrifices in regard
to Vietnam ... were ever given their
just dues.

Rabel: They are Vietnam veterans at an
outreach center in Atlanta, veterans
still trying to come to grips with their
war. For them, the era of self-doubt is
not over. For them, no heartfelt
appreciation for their sacrifices.
Lindsey Roux remembered, and Raoul

Reyes, and Demory Williams—all good American names. It was a week to remember.

Vietnam veteran Emory Williams: You know, you were fighting VC's in Nam; then you came back here, fighting yippies and ... and razzmatazzes, and all them weirdos, you know. And they were ... you were on the front line again. I was ashamed to come back in my uniform. I thought, "Me?" You know. "Aw, no." I told the story before. *(Laughter)* "Me, a silver suit?" And it was December when I got home.

Vietnam veteran Buddy Rentz: You come back here and there's nothing for you. And after 10 or 12 years and you're still fumbling around, you're saying, "Jesus, man, I'm no good. I'm ..." Well, I can't get a job. When you do work, you don't work that long. I drank a lot. I got a drug problem. I got marital problems. Why can't I be like everybody else? Why can't I have what's coming to me?

Max Cleland: I think that those who served this country in uniform during the Vietnam era probably served it out of faith, when it was most difficult to do so. You know, the soldier signs up. And the soldier has to believe. Or the soldier is drafted, and he has to believe. You don't sign on just for the first half of the ball game to see how the score's going to go, and then

94

you're going to bug out the third quarter.

Rabel: Max Cleland was in charge of the Veterans Administration under Jimmy Carter. He lost both legs and an arm in the Vietnam War.

Cleland: That was a terrible problem, where Vietnam … you saw the troops committed and the country sat back and wondered, "Well, let's see. I mean, did we really do this?" You know. Meanwhile, guys are dying out there every day. You … you can't … you can't do that, because when they come home, then everybody says, "Well, sorry coach! You know, we changed the rules in the middle of the game. And, you know, that's the way it goes."

Rabel: Lincoln said this. Abraham Lincoln said this at Gettysburg. "From these honored dead we take increased devotion to that cause for which they gave the last full measure of devotion, that we here highly resolve that these dead shall not have died in vain." The long, bloody war in Vietnam took at least 57,000 American lives. Twenty-five hundred Americans are still missing. These were wounded.

Vietnam veteran Bob Lacy: See, all the times of the hospitals I've been in … this is going to cover twelve years … there wasn't one psychiatrist, one doctor, that ever asked me what happened to me in Vietnam. I mean, that's covering a whole hell of lot of people. Only 'til I got to this center did they start in dealing with that thing.... I feel that my country has let all of us down, in not recognizing us for the warriors that we were.

Vietnam veteran Danny Parker: Well, I ... I killed three children by accident one time that we ... when I was going through a village. And ... and I've got to deal with this. It's ... it ...my... my uncle and his family knows about it anyway, because of a little magazine article, but ... I mean, to turn the basket over and ... and I see these three children. And I have three children now that are the same ages as them ... they were. I figured out the reason that I'm alive today was because I didn't stop and think. People who stopped and thought were dead.

Rabel: It is difficult here at Gettysburg or at any cemetery where warriors are buried to think of anything but the waste and futility of war. ... Carl Sandburg said, "Pile the bodies high at Austerlitz and Waterloo. Shovel them under and let me work. I am the grass; I cover all. And pile them high at Gettysburg. Shovel them under and let me work. I am the grass. Let me work."

More than 6,000 Americans are dead and buried, killed in war in Iraq and Afghanistan. Thirty thousand were wounded and, like the dead, are being forgotten. America no longer views them as heroes, if it ever did, when they come home. As their brothers and sisters from the Vietnam era, too many of the hundreds of thousands who served in our most recent wars are drug addicts and alcoholics—war-related afflictions America tends to forget at war's end.

On February 8, 1981, on *Sunday Morning*, I reported on how badly Americans were treating soldiers returning from Vietnam. Spit upon, harassed, called baby killers; all the soldiers wanted was a little respect. Here is what I said to end the report:

> The Vietnam veterans believe there was never enough embracing, never enough caring. America turned its face away from them. Americans do not suffer defeat gladly, and Vietnam was a defeat. It was a war that went too long, a war that Americans finally realized they never wanted. There were no heroes; there were only victims—the dead and all those who fought in it and their families.

In 2011, the troops came home from Iraq. In 2014, the soldiers are set to depart Afghanistan, leaving the war there in the hands of a corrupt and discredited government put in place by America.

The wars in Iraq and Afghanistan, with their more than 6,000 U.S. dead, have taken their toll. These are wars that went too long, wars Americans finally realized they never wanted. There are no heroes; there are only victims—the dead and all those who fought in it and their families.

16
Vietnam, Laos and Rats

*You can kill ten of my men for every one I kill of yours,
but even at those odds, you will lose and I will win.*
—Ho Chi Minh to the French, late 1940s

More than 2,000,000 Vietnamese died in the war with America. That, of course, doesn't count those killed when the French military tried to hold onto its former colony. The French were vanquished at Dien Bien Phu, where the Viet Minh bloodied them so badly they threw in the towel. Let America fight this unwinnable war, the losers moaned. After all, American warriors pulled French chestnuts out of the fire during World War I, known as the Great War. We did the same in World War II.

So the United States took up the truncheon. We muddled around out there, saw 55,000 of our troops killed in combat and spent untold billions of dollars of national treasure confronting Soviet puppets and Communism. After more than 10 years of fighting, the U.S. exited Vietnam, humiliated by the Soviet-backed Vietcong insurgents and North Vietnam's tank-led, uniformed army. It was a huge military and foreign policy blunder. But President Dwight David Eisenhower said if we didn't stop the commies in Vietnam, the rest of the countries out there would drop like dominoes. Hence the "domino theory," disproved at the expense of the hawks who were sure Vietnam was going to hell in a handbag if we pulled out. The dominoes are still standing. And the U.S. has normal trade and diplomatic relations with communist Hanoi. Then why can't the U.S. normalize relations with Cuba? I'll answer that question later.

For now, let me tell you how it was in 1970 when America's war in Vietnam had overshadowed America's civil rights conflict. If the struggle for the hearts and minds of the South was about to be victorious, the battle for democracy in Vietnam was about to become a lost cause. For 14 months, from November 1969 through January 1971, I went into combat all over South Vietnam to gauge the direction, if any, the U.S. was headed. Being "in country" for more than a year gave me plenty of time to check out the course America was on to subdue Communism in the Cold War fight with the Soviet Union.

The Soviet-backed North Vietnam and the Vietcong insurgents in South Vietnam were the proxy enemies. But they were not ineffective by any means. In 1968, 85,000 Vietcong guerrillas and North Vietnamese soldiers shattered the myth that the U.S. was winning and there was "light at the end of the tunnel." On January 31, the first day of Tet, the Lunar New Year, a well-coordinated, surprise uprising hammered scores of cities and towns and hamlets all over the country. In Saigon, "enemy" rebels penetrated the U.S. Embassy compound and, just before a rescue force arrived, came within minutes of overwhelming the diplomats inside and capturing the Embassy itself. The Tet offensive was a military failure for Hanoi. But it was a political and psychological victory for the Marxists, because it dramatically contradicted claims by the U.S. government the war was all but over.

On his February 27 broadcast, Walter Cronkite presented an editorial opinion saying: "...the bloody experience of Vietnam is to end in a stalemate." Watching Cronkite's broadcast, President Lyndon Johnson is quoted as saying, "That's it. If I've lost Cronkite, I've lost middle America."

President Johnson had opted for limited warfare. War, waged imperfectly, will pulverize the war-makers every time. It makes little sense, to me, not to use everything in a nation's arsenal immediately, without pause, once the decision to resort to war has been made. Maybe that's why I'm not in the army.

Mr. Johnson thought he could win on the cheap without suffering political indignation. He underestimated the enemy, viewing the Vietnamese as if they were children playing soldier for entertainment. He either didn't know about the 400-year-old history of successful combat that defined the Vietnamese, or he ignored the annals.

Either way, the president chose not to have respect for the likes of North Vietnam General Vo Nguyen Giap, who masterminded America's military defeat, the first such defeat ever for the United States. He had crushed the French at Dien Bien Phu. And he would rout America at Saigon in 1975.

Johnson did, finally, commit divisions and armor and bombs, but he did so slowly, with agonizing results. One-by-one, day-by-day, young Americans were picked off in plain sight of ABC and CBS and NBC—my networks, my reporting. Instead of victory, American television audiences saw a humiliating defeat in the making. That gave Americans plenty of time to make up their minds about how their commander-in-chief, President Lyndon Baines Johnson, was conducting the armed campaign. From their armchairs in front of their television sets, there came a resounding thumbs-down.

Commander-in-Chief Johnson might have avoided his disgrace by invoking the military doctrine promulgated by General Colin Powell three decades later in Iraq. Powell was a lowly lieutenant in Vietnam, where he had a front row seat at America's disgraceful stage show. *Never again*, I can imagine Powell thinking.

Two decades later, when Powell became Chairman of the Joint Chiefs of Staff at the Pentagon, he gave invaluable advice to his boss, President George Herbert Walker Bush. Out of that advice the Powell Doctrine was born. Powell insisted that if the nation were going to war in Iraq that it not go there half-heartedly. All of Bush's horses and all of Bush's men had to be employed. Overwhelming military force must be used, Powell asserted, to win the day. And with the help of allied forces, the United States became a proud military power once again. In a three-day blitzkrieg using massive firepower and diversion, Saddam Hussein was ousted from Kuwait and exposed as the fraud he was.

In the fight for victory in Iraq, Powell did not have to worry that a Soviet Union might come to the aid of Saddam. Not so the Marxists in Vietnam. Johnson and his military planners constantly worried the Communist Chinese and the Communist Soviets might go to war alongside their Vietnamese allies. By escalating the war slowly (and painfully), Johnson thought he could obtain victory while staving off the other superpowers. If he had used nuclear weapons against Hanoi, as some hawks were advising, he risked World War III.

By using conventional forces little by little over tortuous years of fighting, Johnson invited a shameful defeat. His strategy was sort of like taking aspirin to trounce cancer. You might feel good for a little while. But in the end, you will die.

By the time I arrived in Vietnam, President Johnson had bowed out of the presidency over the failure in Vietnam. In a surprise on-air announcement, he had told a national TV audience he would not seek a second term. Vietnam had defeated the 36th President of the United States.

Vowing not to allow Vietnam to beat him, Richard Nixon ran for the presidency on the false promise he had a secret plan to conclude the war. There was no secret plan. Mr. Nixon, as president, aggressively pursued a military solution. He invaded Cambodia to "interdict" the bases and trails North Vietnam used to mount attacks against South Vietnam. The failed invasion drew international reproach. Under pressure, Mr. Nixon and his national security advisor, Henry Kissinger, plotted a plan to allow the U.S. to break out of the Southeast Asia quagmire "with honor." They came up with something called "Vietnamization."

Vietnamization was the failed, crafty slight-of-hand policy that President George W. Bush borrowed to get America out of Afghanistan. The Obama administration adopted the same policy. I'll say it again: It didn't work then, and it won't work today.

Take a look at what happened in Laos during Lam Son 719, a combined U.S.-Vietnam operation in February 1971, to cut off and destroy North Vietnamese military units moving south along the Ho Chi Minh trail. Vietcong and North Vietnam regular forces operating in South Vietnam depended on the trail or Route 9 in Laos for resupply of such necessities as arms and ammunition.

The plan: The U.S. Army would use its helicopters to ferry thousands of South Vietnamese troops into neighboring Laos from the infamous Khe Sanh air strip in the highlands near North Vietnam. By using American choppers, the U.S. military could maintain plausible deniability, refuting reports America had boots on the ground in Laos. In other words, this was not an invasion of a sovereign country by the United States. South Vietnam's 1st Cavalry and 1st Rangers group would do the dirty work. The operation ended in disaster.

Bloodied by North Vietnamese artillery and tanks, some of South Vietnam's battalions lost 80 percent of their soldiers. They were no match for the advancing North Vietnamese. Didn't the French teach us anything? So horrific was their retreat that many could be seen in mid-air hanging onto the skids of the American helicopters that went to the rescue. We filmed chopper after chopper returning from the Laotian battlefield with young, terrified Vietnamese clinging to anything they could hang onto in the airborne action. American helicopter pilots, their faces cut up by enemy fire during initial efforts to save the Vietnamese, refused to fly back into Laos.

Fresh American Army helicopter pilots were brought in to make the treacherous raids. The youngsters, barely of shaving age, were put to the test by superior officers on the eve of their dreadful incursion into enemy territory. You might think of the test as a form of fraternity hazing. Each failure to perform a series of complicated hand slapping resulted in beer forcing—forcing a can of beer down the throat of each kid who had failed. They were laughing and drinking and crying, all at the same time. Massive ground fire awaited them in Laos, and they knew it. By the end of the evening of their induction into the assemblage of the damned, the newbies, as they were called, were pissed as rats.

To cap off the evening, older officers sang a song to their young charges. Using "Camptown Races" as the melody, the older men serenaded the kids with this ghoulish song: "You're going home in a body bag, doo dah, doo dah; you're going home in a body bag all the doo dah day."

I supposed, at that moment, President Nixon's plan to let Vietnam do it was stillborn. On the tube, I reported that much to the American people, but apparently nobody was listening or they dismissed my reports as the ranting of a cynic. Later I did stories, prior to 9/11, warning the TV audience about a dangerous man named Osama bin Laden—to no avail. Extremely frustrating. The frustration I felt overwhelmed me at times. I knew the world from a personal perspective; my boots were on the ground. But all my words, all my televised pieces, did nothing to change perceptions by people who could have done something about the threat.

17
Vietnamization

When the President does it, that means that it is not illegal.
—Richard Milhous Nixon

As absurd as "doo dah, doo dah" may have seemed, the Vietnam experience, set in the country's utterly stunning geography, continued to surprise me at every turn. In 1970-71, my base of operations was in Saigon, now Ho Chi Minh City, which was once a pearl of the Orient owned by the French.

I rented an apartment in a building constructed by the French during their old colonial days. The French connection was evident everywhere in Saigon, where fine restaurants serving excellent cuisine competed for the attention of the sophisticated Franco-Asians who were the formation of a lively café society. The old French colonial city would vanish after the war, falling beneath a rapidly rising skyline that would conceal the city's French influences. The new city has a charm all its own.

I found nothing charming, though, about the impositions with which the war burdened Saigon, especially along its wide boulevards. Before dawn on various mornings I awoke hearing earsplitting chugs made by motorbikes that clogged the avenue in front of my place. Mingled with the incessant roar of the bikes were the thumps caused by military helicopters overhead and the cries of street vendors hawking their wares—including live, squawking chickens and squealing piglets.

CBS paid for housing and gave me laundry money, which I used to hire a maid. Maids worked for next to nothing, a fortune in Saigon. The magnanimous chap that I was, I supplemented her income out of my own pocket. The truth is my maid was worth her weight in gold—for more reasons than the cooking, cleaning and laundry she did.
She did all those things, usually arriving just after dawn, carrying the fresh catch of the day. She allowed the lobsters and crabs to crawl about the kitchen floor before sounding the death knell. Shrimp had to stay on the counter until the live lobsters had suffered loss of life in one of the boiling pots assigned to them. The crabs took up their own, separate final assignments on the stove. Lunch was about to be served.

Her greatest service to me was imparted knowledge. I could not prove it, but she was a Vietcong agent for sure. I'll bet she was a clandestine colonel in the NVA. Nothing occurred in Saigon that blindsided my spy. "Do not go to the market today, Mistel Labor," she instructed one day. Good instruction, because a bomb exploded in the market that day, killing and maiming many.

Her ancestry was Chinese, and she lived in the Chinese sector of Saigon, called Cholon. In Cholon restaurants waiters would walk little monkeys to dining tables and seat them in a special chair that held them tightly while a horizontal guillotine decapitated them so patrons immediately could use their chopsticks to pick at their hot brains as the monkeys screamed to high heaven. Another delicacy was dogs. They ate dogs just like your adorable poodles and collies. I never went over there.

Colonel maid used my phone to call her sisters in Cholon when she needed help. She cried for help any time I informed her that within two hours I would be bringing a dozen hungry newsmen to lunch. The geniuses that she and her sisters were, they would serve all of us right on time with 12 separate dishes and one more for good luck. If only I could have brought her home.

The noise of the street was something I did not want to bring home. The hawking and squawking and squealing formed harsh harmonics. They put a coda on the brash symphony of the piercing sounds the Vietnamese make when their strange idiom opens up in full force like dogs and ducks engaged in mortal battle. And then there were the rats. Or, as Indiana Jones would say, "Rats, it had to be rats." Or was it snakes?

One of them, looking like a furry boxer bulldog, peered right into my eyes that opened in a flash when it fell into my bedroom, a place for slumber ordinarily. The inconsiderate wakening developed into full-fledged fear as the overgrown mouse sat there, motionless, challenging my terrified gaze. Just as I reached for my pistol the great big varmint darted this way and that looking for a way out. The thing must have known intuitively I was about to fill it full of lead. Just as I was keen to pull the trigger, it bounded up the wall and out one of the openings the French had cut out for ventilation. Luckily for the rat, it hadn't been ventilated by me on the way out.

I reported the speedy spectacle of the scrounger to my maid when she arrived later that morning. She calmly advised me to just leave it alone if it came back. It would leave on its own, she said. "Ho Do jeh," (pronounced ho-tou-yeh), I said, thanking her in heavily English-accented Chinese. I was grateful for any advice she gave me. I wish she had had some advice for me on my once-a-month assignment in Da Nang, hundreds of miles north.

In the after hours, we gathered in a Da Nang bar to celebrate another day of survival. We were young, too.

Cameramen and reporters and producers, hangers on and free-lancers, all trying to forget or remember the position we were in. It was not a pretty position.

The open-air saloon, overlooking the Da Nang River, had a chicken-wire defense against grenades that were often thrown from the street below. Vietcong cowboys, as they were called, rode their motorcycles down there and pitched their "frags" at us. Being in the bar was chancy.

One day, one of the cowboys rode up close beside me to snatch from my wrist the expensive watch I was wearing. They were apt to do that when they weren't hurling bombs in our direction. I, too, was astraddle a motorcycle on my way to the bar. Both of us were speeding down the street on our cycles when the bandit lunged at me, clawing to rip me off. He grabbed my wristwatch but managed only to make me snap the handle-bar of my motorbike. My body, the bike and my watch spilled into the middle of Da Nang's notorious rush hour traffic. Just as in Saigon, rush hour went from 5 a.m. 'til midnight, strangling everyone in sight with clouds of billowing smoke from the thousands of belching bikes that jammed the roadways.

I jumped up from the attack, somewhat bloody, to see the escaping robber look back in disappointment over his failure to part me from my timepiece and, possibly, my life. I hoisted my precious, dependable clock and screamed, "Maybe next time, motherfucker!"

Back at the bar, the sing-song melodies of the Vietnamese language permeated the night air. Aging Vietnamese prostitutes wore bulging Ao Dais which only pretty, slim girls should wear. To those of you who have never had tumescence incited by the very sight of that cunning attire, I will now define for you the awe-inspiring Ao Dai. It is a long (usually white) tunic worn over loose fitting trousers (usually black) by Vietnamese women (and some pretenders) that has a high neck and is slit at both sides below the waist. Clad in this wantonly sexual outfit, Vietnamese women with long shimmering black hair can drive a man, and some other women, crazy.

The plump oldsters sporting their tunics, fit to bust, sat at some of the tables in the bar, watching intently the huge rats that scurried about. My covert colonel maid was nowhere to be found, still in Saigon, I supposed. I had a feeling the rats had come for me, led by the one that had fallen on me in Saigon. These were fat rats, bigger than fat cats, feeling at home, and there was an unexplained intimacy between the rats and the whores. The rats appraised us suspiciously with beady, red, gleaming eyes. So did the prostitutes.

In the background, a beautiful Vietnamese songstress was doing her best to imitate a popular American song: "I want some led loses for a bruerady," she sang.

My superb cameraman, Greg Cooke, couldn't take it anymore. I think his mind snapped. He fled from the bar to fashion something with which to murder the vermin that had invaded our space. And I don't mean the women of the night.

He grabbed an empty, metal 16 mm film canister (about the size of a Frisbee) and filled it with stones. It was a formidable weapon. Greg sneaked in, out and around the pillars that held up the roof to get his best shot. Then he launched the missile at the running rats, cackling as he did so.

The rats were stunned, as were the whores. "Why you do that?" they implored. "Why you do that? They are our friends! We feed them!" *Time to ask for the check*, I thought.

President Nixon was thinking the same thing. But it would take four years and 20,000 more American soldiers killed before it would all be over. Instead of exiting immediately and, therefore, saving hundreds of thousands of lives on both sides, the Nixon team chose a political solution to save face. Vietnamization saved face, killed a bunch of people and let the U.S. simply throw up its hands and leave without ever admitting the big lie.

Gideon Rose, editor of Foreign Affairs, was more charitable. In a June 2011 opinion piece for *The New York Times*, Rose wrote this: "Richard M. Nixon and his national security adviser, Henry A. Kissinger, tried to manage the risks of exiting the Vietnam War by masking their withdrawal with deliberate deception..."

18
The Five O' Clock Follies

I don't think people want to hear about Vietnam.
I think it was destined for failure simply because [it isn't] a
funny war.
—TV Network Executive

Nowhere was Mr. Nixon's cover-up more evident than at
the so-called Five O'clock Follies in Saigon. I covered the
Follies as part of my adventure in Vietnam. Every afternoon
at five o'clock, Army spokesmen appeared before a gaggle
of reporters to mostly lie. That was their job. They lied by
saying the U.S. was winning. They lied by saying the South
Vietnam military was ready to take over the war. And they
lied by saying "Vietnamization" was working.

The eight-year-old Saigon spectacle had its final
performance with an all-American cast. Army Major Jere
Forbus, the last Follies star, said with a sigh, "Well, we may
not have been perfect, but we outlasted *Fiddler on the
Roof.*"

Mr. Nixon's strategy lasted long enough to get himself out
of hot water politically, but it produced a prolonged,
disrespectful departure. It had been designed to look like
the U.S. was getting out of the predicament without panic.
Or, as Gideon Rose put it in his 2011 *New York Times* op
ed, "…without turning a retreat into a rout."

But U.S. military officers in charge of Vietnamization knew
the exit policy was a farce. Today, those charged with
getting out of the war in Afghanistan fear the U.S. is
heading toward the same kind of rout. They won't say so.

That's called a lie of omission. The Five O'clock Follies have been transferred from Saigon to Washington.
By 2014, Mr. Obama has promised, all our soldiers will come home. Mr. Obama's military are carrying water for the president by supporting Afghanization, just as the mouthpieces for Mr. Nixon supported Vietnamization.

Losing in Afghanistan and Iraq, military experts believe, will put American armed forces in a depressing spiral downward, just like the aftermath of Vietnam. U.S. credibility throughout the region will be vanquished completely by the failed mission. Terrorism will skyrocket. Pakistan will solidify its position as a rogue state in possession of nuclear weapons. We will be sorry for the humiliating retreat. That bad ending is not something the White House talks about openly.

In his op-ed Rose wrote, "The first rule of withdrawal [from Afghanistan] is you do not talk about withdrawal. You may agree with the doves about the value of exiting, but you should respect the hawks' fears about what will happen once people realize what you are doing. You must deflect attention from the true state of affairs, doing everything you can to keep your foes and even your friends in the dark as long as possible." I believe he was right.

19
The Uses of Patriotism

Patriotism is the last refuge of a scoundrel.
—Samuel Johnson, 1775

When reporters call them out for dishonesty, the U.S. military usually respond with a force-five storm of anger. The military have very long memories.

Twenty-three years after I did a controversial story about Army nurses in Vietnam, the Pentagon had not forgotten. In 1993, I reported for permanent duty at the Pentagon as the NBC correspondent. The officer in charge of Army P.R., my amigo, Major General Charles W. "Bill" McClain, Jr., confronted me, wrongly accusing me of broadcasting the identity of an Army lieutenant the American Army nurses were tending at a MASH (Mobile Army Surgical Hospital) in Quang Tri Province, South Vietnam. Remember, this was 23 years after the fact.

The first rule of reporting on America's wars is that reporters may never reveal combat plans in advance of an operation. Second, they must not disclose identities of those killed or wounded in combat until relatives have been notified. Cameraman Cooke, killer of rats, never shot a frame of film of the wounded lieutenant's face, nor did I divulge his name. But the drama of the story exposed vividly the suffering of a young American who had lost his arm to a land mine and was begging the nurses and surgeons not to remove any more of his mangled extremities. As the nurses tried to keep him alive, the lieutenant could be heard pleading, "I have given you my arm, please don't take my legs."

The heroes in that surgical hospital in 1970 were the nurses who kept the lieutenant alive and saved his legs. The young women about to lose their innocence were confronted with the wounds of war that hurt them deeply and for all time, in their minds and souls. Day after day, medevac helicopters brought the freshly slain and injured to their doorstep. The modern day Nightingales received their bleeding and punctured and broken patients with open arms, their tears flowing into the wounds they had to bind up. At another time and in another place, the youngsters, ruined men and ruined women, might have been lovers of another kind. But the intimacy shared by them in the hospital was born of a need far greater than a simple act of carnality. Their affection transcended all love-making. Deeper, more profound feeling fused the soldiers and their caretakers in a mutual adoration of selflessness and pity.

The nurses had volunteered for their duty. At their induction, stateside, they were educated in the theory of war and its losses. Nothing could prepare them, though, for what they faced in reality at Quang Tri. Nowhere else could the intensity of the madness of war be observed in one place, in the premature lines that crisscrossed their youthful faces, in the eyes opened wide in permanent dismay.

Women should not be exposed to such terror that bloody battle inflicts on the observer and participant. Neither should men. If it were a benign world, nature would give birth only to eternal purity that is never corrupted by a mankind bathed in free will. Our self-awareness does us no good. We do with it what we may, and we may destroy ourselves.

The war destroyed the men brought in on stretchers. The war destroyed the women who picked them up off the stretchers and placed them in their own caring custody.

And they could not let go. Images of legless and armless men they patched up would haunt them forever. Mangled bodies of fallen warriors—men their own age—would nightmare them into oblivion.

The women—girls really—tried to put the war out of mind at a pristine beach just below the MASH. They stripped off their bloody scrubs and put on scanty bikinis that kept no secrets from prying eyes. Waves of water introduced themselves as the South China Sea, rolling up onto the sand and tickling tiny toes with nails painted in various shades of magenta. A glorious Montana-blue sky had, somehow, migrated from West to East and allowed its blazing sun to bathe the beauties in erotic repose. Throbbing sexuality oozed from every pore of their bodies, radiating like a mirage into an overheated atmosphere.

If anybody wanted to dismiss the massacres and other gory insights into depravity occurring just a few miles away, this was the place to do it. But a scary deliveryman invariably swooped down upon them and transfixed them with his cargo of the dead and badly wounded. The beachgoers scattered like a flock of seabirds frightened into frenzied flight. The flap, flap, flap of helicopter blades beat down upon them, urging them away from their sandy fantasy and into their real world of blood bags and drip tubes. Once again their escape plan had been foiled.

A popular prime time television series called *China Beach* would be adapted from my broadcast, "Nurses at Quang Tri." The adaptation attempted to grasp the poignancy of the story the nurses told to me, but the series would never do them justice. And by the way, in the TV show *MASH*, "Hot Lips" Houlihan never came close. My original story found its way onto Walter Cronkite's 1985 video tape and DVD series, *The Vietnam War—Courage Under Fire*. But no camera could ever capture the dreadful internal feelings that suffused the women. No amount of telling could exorcise the secret agony they would carry for the rest of their lives. They never really wanted any of the ugliness the war spit out daily, hourly, without end. If they had it to do over again, the nurses told me "no way." And there was no way to make it up to them, not in a million years.

Such reporting from Vietnam undermined the Nixon strategy by boosting cries by the doves and many others in America for the U.S. to exit immediately. If you were anti-war, then, your protest got on the air. That was news. Accordingly, hawks in America wrapped themselves in the flag and questioned the patriotism of those of us who paid attention to the likes of Jane Fonda, "Hanoi Jane," the ultimate bomb thrower.

At the time, the military sought to negate my reporting by attacking me for breaking the rules. The facts: we did not identify the patient and did not show his face.

Reporting is a lonely profession when, at the outset, you are perceived to be wrong, knowing full well history will prove you right. No banners fly for you then, no trumpets blare to honor your insight. After all, you are just doing your job. In honor of that profound virtue, I woke up one recent morning with an unusual thought running around in my brain, circling incessantly and urging my vocal chords to spring into action. Out came the theory like an oral catharsis: If you have wronged the wronged, you are not entitled to right the righteous. No matter how great one thinks it is, he has no right to promote his own agenda by knowingly disparaging another's opinion with which he happens to disagree. Such mischief occurs all the time, in the military, in politics and in life generally. Standing up for your own beliefs works without putting down another's. Men and women I know in the media are not satisfied simply with their own success. They often see to it that others get no satisfaction in their triumphs. Sick, but true.

A nationwide draft outraged much of the country. The military inducted 18-year-olds, without their permission, to die by the thousands in an alien place. Sons and brothers and fathers were being killed in a war that most of them did not approve. The all-volunteer force was born out of the innate unfairness of the draft that commandeered poor blacks, whites and Hispanics while granting deferment to the more privileged. Dick Cheney did not serve. Nor did George W. Bush. Nor did William Jefferson Clinton. Nor did Edward Lawrence Rabel, Jr.

All of those in the U.S. military today volunteer to serve. There is no draft now. Maybe the draft caused the Vietnam defeat. Or was it the fact this was America's first living-room war, bad news on the doorstep day after day? I don't know for sure.

In 1993, young officers at the Army War College in Carlsburg, Pennsylvania, took me to task for the MASH story that was aired on the *CBS Evening News* with Cronkite when they were still in diapers. They had invited me to their school to speak to their classes on my point of view. My story about the nurses and the wounded lieutenant was fresh in their minds even though it aired at a time when the injured lieutenant could have been their father.

Still, following my speeches to their classes, the fresh-faced kids in uniform recounted, vividly, every aspect of the nurses' story. Not only did they viciously take me to task for allegedly violating military rules not to identify wounded, they blamed me and the media in general for the war's ignominious end. Passed through the lore of the corps, handed down from generation to generation of officers,

117

such stories become the legacy of treason in their minds. The military have long memories.

20
Peter Arnett

Give me the liberty to know, to utter, and to argue
freely according to conscience, above all liberties.
—John Milton, *Areopagitica* (1644)

A special mission envelops good journalists when they charge themselves with taking on the world to root out evil, and Peter Arnett is a good journalist. Although he was caught up accidentally in the thin patina of glamour that tops off television reporting these days, Peter committed himself to his life-long search for the truth that would set men free. For his dedication, his career was shattered.

My friend and Pulitzer Prize winner Peter Arnett can tell you all about the wrath the White House and Pentagon unleashed on him. In the human failing that afflicts all of us, Peter was no different. Usually there is forgiveness when something goes wrong, but the Pentagon never forgives or forgets. In 1998, Peter narrated a long television story on CNN entitled *The Valley of Death.* The report claimed the United States Army used deadly Sarin gas against a group of deserting U.S. soldiers in Laos in 1970. The combatants allegedly involved belonged to an elite Green Beret A-Team. The report was expressly approved by both CNN Chairman Tom Johnson and my old friend and producer Rick Kaplan, who was president of CNN at the time.

Angered over the report it deemed deeply flawed, the Pentagon commissioned another account contradicting CNN and Arnett. The 12-man Special Forces team were wounded in action during Operation Tailwind, which had absolutely nothing to do with Sarin gas, according to the

Pentagon version of what happened. Heads rolled at CNN. Co-producers of the CNN report, April Oliver and Jack Smith, were dismissed. Oliver and Smith, in turn, sued Time Warner, the parent company of CNN, claiming they had been wrongfully fired. Time Warner ultimately paid millions of dollars to settle their lawsuits, along with other suits brought by military personnel who claimed to have been libeled in the CNN story.

The Pentagon was not satisfied. It reportedly applied extreme demands on CNN, threatening to withdraw any and all cooperation with the cable network if Peter were not let go. CNN Pentagon correspondent Jamie McIntyre confirmed for me the Pentagon action. In a quote on the World Socialist Web Site, producer Oliver said: "His [Arnett's] firing was a direct result of Pentagon pressure. Perry Smith [a retired USAF major general and former CNN consultant] told *The Wall Street Journal* last July that CNN would not get cooperation from the Pentagon unless Peter Arnett was fired. … They will do anything to stem the flow of information."

Whatever the case, Peter's journalism career was shattered in the episode. He had been brought low by the military for an alleged action that categorized the Pentagon with Nazi Germany in gassing its own troops.

Arnett had worked for *National Geographic* magazine, and later for various television networks, most notably CNN. He was well known for his coverage of war, including the Vietnam War and the Gulf War. He was awarded the 1966 Pulitzer Prize in International Reporting for his work in Vietnam, where he was present from 1962 to 1975, most of the time reporting for The Associated Press news agency. In 1994, Arnett wrote *Live from the Battlefield: From Vietnam to Baghdad, 35 Years in the World's War Zones*. In March 1997, one year before his report about Sarin gas,

Arnett interviewed Osama bin Laden. Arnett was at the top of his profession. The Journalism School at the Southern Institute of Technology is named after him.

The only thing any of us journalists has left in life is our reputation. Great care must be taken when putting our stamp of approval, our byline, on any piece of information we transmit as the gospel. Dan Rather's failure to get it right doomed him. So it was with Arnett. And so it was with me at *Quang Tri*. However, when I was put on the Pentagon beat by NBC, I requested that the Army review the matter. Upon investigation they concluded that I had gotten the story right and had not revealed the name. No matter. I always had to remember to not step out of line.

21
Lessons of a Failed War

But war's a game, which, were their subjects wise, Kings would not play at.
—William Cowper

Testing the veracity of "Vietnamization," I accompanied South Vietnamese troops into a rubber plantation in Cambodia at Snoul in May 1970. The old French plantation was just 90 miles north of Saigon. The North Vietnamese Vietcong Fifth Division aimed to capture the strategic town located only about 10 miles from the Vietnam-Cambodia border. From there the mechanized division could strike at the heart of Vietnam and attack U.S. troops in a blitzkrieg to Saigon. At about 2:30 in the morning I was startled out of a thin slumber by a flurry of machine gun fire. Then the mortars started coming in. *Whump, whump, whump*, the incoming getting closer and closer. White hot metal slammed into the I-beams behind which we had been trying to grab some sleep when the attack began. Cries from the wounded and dying South Vietnamese soldiers competed with the loud sounds and scenes of war.

Cameraman Mike Marriott was filming what he could. There had been hours, days of boredom before the timeline was broken instantaneously by the sharp crack of the inbound killers. So far we had survived, but the fear of the imminent ground attack was greater than the event itself. Marriott and I knew from experience we would not survive the fanatic Vietcong and North Vietnam regulars, backed up by tanks and running at us from many directions.

The South Vietnamese were not up to the task of turning back the enemy. The ARVN, or Army of South Vietnam, had failed before, and we knew it would fail this time. Why test people who were known to be bound for failure? Their refusal to fight effectively was due to their lack of devotion to their corrupt government in Saigon. They weren't fighting for their country. However, the uncompromising band of warriors coming at us did have something to fight for, and they were about to prove it. We were just about to be overrun by screaming throngs bullied on by blaring bugles.

The night sky blazed with flares that could illuminate a square mile of "Charlies" just before they put your lights out. Scalding red and white tracer bullets crisscrossed right before my eyes, making my throat parch out of panic and desperation. My mind began the invariable descent into unreality wherein the approaching doom is transformed into "The Dance of the Sugar Plum Fairies," just before shock and blackness take you out of the action.

Myriad remembrances mess up the mind before black-out, like the pictures taken and stored along the way when the troops we followed nonchalantly rode into the plantation on their armored personnel carriers, live chickens and piglets acting as rear guard. Freshly slaughtered pigs and grilled pork chops and the white meat of chicken beat out American-style C-rations every time. Foul-smelling Vietnamese fish sauce called *Nướcmắm* had worked as the perfect condiment for the plantation feast served up right before the shit hit the fan.

My reverie was splintered abruptly by the brrrrrrrrrrrr of a minigun firing almost 4,000 bullets per minute at the advancing North Vietnamese. An American AC-130 "Spooky" gunship orbited right above me, using 105mm, 40mm and 25mm munitions to drive back the hordes who wanted my life and the lives of everyone around me.

Lieutenant General Nguyen Van Minh, commanding the South Vietnamese forces in Cambodia, had called for all available United States air support to help keep the enemy division from pushing into South Vietnam. A force identified as the enemy's Seventh Division, west of Snoul, was also attacked. In addition, B-52s reportedly bombed what was believed to be the headquarters of the enemy's Ninth Division on the Chup rubber plantation, 110 miles northwest of Saigon, and 55 miles northeast of Phnom Penh, the Cambodian capital. It was from the Chup plantation that enemy troops moved southward and attacked Cambodian soldiers on the eastern approaches of Phnom Penh.

The battle for Snoul was fought fiercely throughout the night and into the next day. Saigon headquarters said the bodies of 99 enemy soldiers had been counted after the fight, which the Vietnamese said they had won. I counted numerous NVA bodies strewn along Route 7, the main artery leading to Saigon. To keep my sanity in the counting, I visualized the bodies as if they were dolls not to be taken seriously. By acting as if I were in a movie and the dolls would stand up and go about their business after I had passed by left me with a semblance of reason and hope. But maybe I am still kidding myself into believing I was not maddened by the exposure to the madness and I may be carrying the craziness with me to this very day.

Marriott, who was out of the tradition of the fine Australian photographers on our staff, said the battles for Snoul were "as bad as it gets." And the veteran Asia hand had seen many battles. Aerial observers estimated an additional 120 NVA soldiers had been killed by U.S. and South Vietnamese air strikes about a mile northeast of Snoul. Body count was all the rage among the commanders. The bigger the body count, the better the chances allied forces

were winning the war. Of course, the body count criterion would be exposed for the farce it was, for our side had suffered severe casualties as well. In the face of the NVA thrusts, the South Vietnamese forces, and we, withdrew from Snoul and were almost wiped out in the retreat.
A spokesman put the South Vietnamese losses during the pullback at six men wounded. But from where we crouched in the field we knew that about 200 of the ARVN had been killed or wounded. Fittingly, the Cambodian spokesman's name was Am Rong. "The withdrawal," the spokesman said, "was part of the whole plan of operation in Cambodia during the rainy season." He said the withdrawal had been "preplanned," adding that government troops had similarly been pulled back from Snoul at the same time the year before as the summer monsoon got underway. I don't remember one drop of rain falling in all the days I was in Snoul.

The government spokesman went on to say there would be further realignments of the South Vietnamese Army positions in Cambodia in preparation for the rainy season. He stressed the government troops who had left Snoul were still in Cambodia. The Associated Press contradicted the government's position, reporting that, according to information from the field, the ARVN had pulled back across the border to Locninh in South Vietnam. And the AP was correct from my point of view. The spokesman denied what had really happened, saying it was possible some battle-damaged South Vietnamese armored personnel carriers, tanks and trucks had been destroyed by government troops in Snoul as the pullout began, rather than letting them fall into enemy hands. But reports from the field, quoted by The Associated Press, said 80 tanks, armored personnel carriers, jeeps and trucks had been left behind by the South Vietnamese, who also reportedly destroyed 12 artillery pieces.

In Washington, Jerry W. Fredham, the Pentagon spokesman, said the South Vietnamese had always intended to withdraw some main combat units from Cambodia with the onset of the rainy season. The withdrawal, he said, "appears from here to be orderly and according to their plan." The truth is, the withdrawal was a rout. And the AP got the rout right with its reporting on May 31, 1970.

SAIGON, South Vietnam, May 31 (AP) - North Vietnamese troops reportedly drove a South Vietnamese task force today from the Cambodian town of Snoul, which United States troops captured more than a year ago. The South Vietnamese apparently were badly battered. Reports from the field said that the Saigon task force of up to 2,000 men fled Snoul with scores of wounded. As they fought their way across Route 13 toward the South Vietnamese border 10 miles to the south, they were reported to be disabling artillery guns and destroying some of their trucks and armored personnel carriers.

Field reports said that the task force had not been resupplied because roads had been washed out by monsoon rains. Many of the vehicles were said to have run out of fuel. There was no firm count on casualties, but it was reported that more than 100 South Vietnamese wounded, some awaiting evacuation several days, had been lifted out of rear areas by both South Vietnamese and United States helicopters.

The retreat from Snoul opens up a supply route for the North Vietnamese, giving them control of portions of Routes 7 and 13 that lead into the northern provinces of South Vietnam's Military Region III. This region includes Saigon and 11 surrounding provinces and shares 231 miles of border with Cambodia. Snoul is 90 miles north of Saigon.

Lieut. Gen. Nguyen Van Minh, commander of Military Region III, said a week ago that his forces were effectively blocking the infiltration of North Vietnamese troops and supplies into the region. General Minh also said that he planned to keep his task forces operating along Route 7 even during the current rainy season. Several other task forces still remain along portions of Route 7 to the west of Snoul and along Route 15, the Saigon-Pnompenh artery.

Two North Vietnamese regiments from the Fifth Division, with up to 4,000 troops, are massed in the Snoul area, according to latest intelligence reports. Two battalions of North Vietnamese troops, as many as 1,000 men, were reported to have attacked Snoul last Wednesday in the heaviest assaults in three months against the South Vietnamese defenders. There has been heavy fighting since then.

Field reports said the remnants of the South Vietnamese armored column retreating toward the border had been attacked by North Vietnamese troops seven miles southeast of Snoul. There were no casualty reports available from the field, but a bulletin from headquarters in Saigon said 54 North Vietnamese troops had been killed and 15 weapons had been captured. The bulletin said 16 South Vietnamese soldiers had been wounded.This appeared in *The New York Times*:

Saigon Denies Rout by Enemy at Snoul
By IVER PETERSON, Special to *The New York Times*

SAIGON, South Vietnam, Wednesday, June 2 - The South Vietnamese task force that withdrew from the eastern Cambodian town of Snoul on Monday is still inside Cambodia, a Saigon spokesman said yesterday. The spokesman, Lieut. Col. Le Trung Hien, denied reports that the Government troops had been driven under heavy attack from the rubber-plantation town, which is 10 miles from the South Vietnamese border and 90 miles north of Saigon. He described the pullout as a "realignment" caused by the coming rainy season and not enemy pressure. He estimated that during the withdrawal more than 700 North Vietnamese troops had been killed by American and South Vietnamese planes and helicopter gunships and by South Vietnamese tanks. The enemy, he said, was attacked along Routes 7 and 13, which were also the lines of the South Vietnamese withdrawal.

In the fog of war, truth is the first casualty.

22
Danielle, My Belle

I will not mourn, although my heart is torn,
Oh, love forever lost! I will not mourn.
—Heinrich Heine

I advanced into Graham Greene's Laos in 1973.It was
Easter in the Christian world, and America had launched its
latest major military offensive in Vietnam. Once again, the
U.S. was failing to wipe out the Communists. Mr. Nixon and
Mr. Kissinger had tried something like this by sending
troops into Cambodia in April 1970, a month before the
battle in Snoul. The invasion of Cambodia provoked a wave
of demonstrations in the United States. In one of them, four
students were killed when National Guardsmen opened fire
at Kent State University. In the days that followed, 450
colleges closed in protest against the killings.

The arrival of U.S. Marines in Cambodia provoked hostility
among the local population. The Cambodian Communist
movement, the Khmer Rouge, had received little support
from the peasants before the United States invasion. Now
the Khmer Rouge was in a position to appeal to nationalist
sentiments by claiming Cambodia was about to be taken
over by the United States. During 1970 and 1971,
membership in the Khmer Rouge grew rapidly.

Laos, another country bordering Vietnam, had also been
attacked; Lam Son 719 was one of the cross border
interdictions. As in Cambodia, this kind of action increased
the support for the communist Pathet Lao. By 1973, the
Pathet Lao controlled most of the country. My goal in Laos
was to uncover and expose the various skirmishes and

other activities going on inside and in between a variety of factions—Air America (CIA) pilots, drug runners, embassy personnel and spies from every agency—including the Russians and Chinese.

The key to penetrating the confusing maze was the great Indochinese Hotelier Maurice Cavalerie. Graham Greene could not have invented a better character for *The Quiet American.* Maurice Cavalerie, not to be confused with Maurice Chevalier unless you want to—and I want to— reminded me of Chevalier singing *Thank Heaven for Little Girls.* His French accented English was Chevalier personified.

"Monsieur Rabel, I woul' like for you to met my daughter, Danielle." And I would, absolutely, like to "met" Danielle, for she was an enchanting young woman with her father's formidable brainpower and her mother's good looks. Cavalerie, the father, wasn't bad looking himself.

The beauteous Danielle and her dad proved utterly invaluable in their assistance to me. They opened doors and arranged interviews and provided insights that otherwise would have been way beyond my reach. For illustration, they interceded on my behalf with the CIA to hitch a ride on one of the agency's airplanes to fly into the poppy fields in the Laotian highlands. The agency airline went by the name of Air America. The single-engine, fixed-wing STOL (short takeoff and landing) aircraft could land on a dime and take off in just about the same distance.

The Cavaleries had to have had some very powerful sway with the CIA to get me on that flight. We landed adjacent to a poppy plantation, where Laotian women went about gathering extract from the bright red flower. The extract is used in the production of a narcotic or medicine. Think dope—millions of dollars in illegal drugs in this case. The

Air America pilot gathered up the product and threw it in the plane, which he navigated back to his Vientiane base. From there the pilot delivered the goods to Cavalerie's famed Constellation Hotel on the Rue Samsentai. I don't know where the stuff went from there—probably into the drug pipeline to the U.S.

Over the course of four decades I have put up in rat holes and sojourned in five-star hotels whose names fall on the ear like music: The Savoy, The Connaught, The Peninsula in Hong Kong, George V in Paris and The Ritz in New York. Most often, I have been in the better class of lodgings on someone else's dime. CBS and NBC also paid for the rat holes.

The Hotel Constellation was in a class all its own. If it weren't for real guests and a real restaurant serving *élevée* gastronomy and *vin superieure*, the place could have served as a movie prop a la *Casablanca*. It was the foreign correspondent's hub, nerve center and sleeping quarters. Cavalerie was our supplier of food, fine wines and anything else we desired before we retired to our green and yellow tiled upstairs bedrooms. He made us feel at ease and was always there to help us.

Cavalerie's biographer writes, "… to survive in this utterly corrupt nation, with all types of foreign agents plotting their secret deals in a deadly power struggle, he must have kowtowed to many sides. Was it the French 'Deuxieme Bureau,' the CIA or the unscrupulous Royal Family, the Pathet Lao, Vietcong or just the deadly Corsican Mafia? ~These French Mafiosi were the movers and shakers, kept [sic] the above and below the line economy going. They were the white washers of huge sums of opium and heroin money traded in—at a profitable commission—for gold bars. They had a hand in every bar, hotel, opium den and whore house in the country."

131

In addition to being a friend to me, Maurice and his clever, nimble daughter were my advisers, intelligence chiefs, moneychangers and experienced travel guides. I delighted in Cavalerie's wry comment, "I never break the law because in Laos everything is legal."

Danielle and I went flying together in one of the CIA's helicopters. She brought some sticky rice, a Laotian snack that chews like candy. We flew over evergreen mountains and swooped into lush mountain valleys that hid our targets from view. We were after the secret places and people that animated our storytelling and revealed the ancient enchantment of the land of 1001 elephants.

Actually, Laos means the *Land of a Million Elephants*. I'm not sure why the country was named for elephants—there aren't that many around. They estimate there are about 500 wild elephants in Laos. Subtract 500 from 1001 and you get 501. Maybe they should call Laos the *Land of 501 Elephants*.

Danielle radiated a mysterious persona, living proof that femininity is way underrated. She had all those bodily charms attributed to the stunning women descending from Asian females and French males who mated during colonization. Visualize Bloody Mary's beautiful daughter, Liat, embracing the American officer Lt. Cable to the sounds of "Younger Than Springtime" on Bali Ha'i in Rogers and Hammerstein's *South Pacific*, and you will possess the scene, pitch perfect. Ah, yes, my fantasy from my ushering days when I was 14 had come true. I had found my Liat.

I was so sentimental then. I am still, as you may have guessed. She was born in Hanoi where, at the time, Maurice thrived as a wealthy and respected member of the French business community. Danielle's grandmother was a teacher, the educated daughter of an aristocratic Chinese family, from the last generation of such ladies to have bound feet. Her grandfather was a botanist from the Massif Central region of France. The Museum of Natural History in Paris sent him to study the plants of southern China, where he met and married Danielle's grandmother.

Maurice attended the Lycee Albert Sarraut in Hanoi to complete his baccalaureate, after which he enrolled in the medical faculty of the University of Hanoi. On the side Maurice traded in commodities like sugar, which were in short supply and high demand in Indochina. At the same time he tutored at the Lycee, where in 1942 he met another young instructor, his bride to be, Rosalie Erembert, Danielle's mother.

By 1973, Danielle was fully formed and full of mischief. She did things to frighten me, but I was never frightened. Her exquisite face altered itself into sadness when I wouldn't play along. Her lips turned downward, and her delightful eyes followed suit when her plaything failed to have fun. For some unknown reason, she referred to me as Superman. But she must have thought I was vulnerable, for she played tricks on me all the time.

One time she tried to trick me into thinking a gecko had landed on my back. A gecko is unique among lizards in its vocalizations, making chirping sounds in social interactions with other geckos. Geckos are the second most species-rich group of lizards (after skinks), with close to 1,500 different species worldwide and many others likely yet to be discovered. They are big, slow and scaly, not like the small, fleeting and slick creatures we are used to. The New Latin *gekko* and English *gecko* stem from the Malay *gēkoq*, which is imitative of the sound the animals make. Geee-echo, geee-echo - eh, eh, eh - geh-co, geh-co, geh-co. Not anywhere as cute as that little green guy on TV with his Australian accent, flogging insurance for Geico.

My playmate threw a piece of bark at my back when I was turned away from her. I seldom turned my back on her because she was such a beauty to see. When the bark hit my back, Danielle cried out, "Geh-co, geh-co, geh-co." I shrugged nonchalantly and glanced backward over my left shoulder with a smile. I shall always remember her brightening face that was just a small measure of her total radiance.

In all the time I was in the magical kingdom that was Laos, Danielle was my entre into forbidden chambers, my translator of hidden languages, and the escape artist who showed me the way. If there was ever to be a breakout because of the transgressions of the enemy, she knew which back alleys to take. Evil was no odd job to be managed after the day's work was done. She cast out demons as if they were old copper pennies. And if at the end of the journey things had gone badly, Danielle was the one who could knit up the raveled sleeve of day.

Suffice to say, without revealing classified information, Danielle intervened to prevent a physical attack on me by anti-American groups in Laos after I revealed embarrassing news about their activities. She also negotiated with friendly forces on my behalf after I exposed them for their secret assassination projects. She was amazing.

On a super-secret helicopter mission to find and rescue a downed American fighter pilot who was in forbidden territory, we were a team. U.S. forces were not supposed to be in Laos at that time, so authorities could not admit the existence of an American pilot's being shot down there. We risked our futures by being aboard the undercover chopper that, if it crashed and burned, its CIA operatives would

134

have denied we ever existed. Unfortunately, we did not find the pilot.

Maurice knew the dangers in the hush-hush undertaking. He was deeply concerned for Danielle's safety. But there was no insurance policy I could provide. The only warranty in the scheme of things was a job well done, a journalist's duty rightfully performed. She was under no obligation to ride with me on the operation. Perhaps because she had arranged the top secret expedition, she felt a responsibility for me. She never said so. She went without qualification. And I loved her for her selflessness.

Danielle had seven siblings, the girls even prettier than she, if you can imagine that. So let us cast imagination aside and provide a fulsome description: She had raven hair that fell below her shoulders onto ivory skin. Dark eyes tore into my soul and ripped apart my pretense. Bewitching lips beckoned for a kiss to satisfy agonizing longing. I could say Danielle was voluptuous in every sense of the word. Her soft curves, in the words of Wooten, did magic to the soul of man. I was therefore puzzled over how she had escaped the advances of the French diplomats and American news correspondents her sisters could not resist. They married themselves off, one-by-one to those foreigners. Unfortunately for me, another Frenchman jumped into our playpen at the last moment and snatched her away.

Adieu, Danielle. Merci pour tout.

23
Somalia

A military operation involves deception.
Even though you are competent, appear to be incompetent.
Though effective, appear to be ineffective.
—Sun-tzu, The Art of War

Commanders in Somalia in 1995 should have known better, having been forewarned by what happened in Snoul, Cambodia, way back in 1970. Back then nobody thought about what to do after the war was over. The U.S. had only one thought in mind: How to get out of Vietnam as fast as possible while keeping the fig leaf of honor in place. The lesson went unlearned.

In retrospect, neither Somalia nor Snoul were worth the risk of life. But when the reporter is 25 years of age, he thinks he is bulletproof. Still, I put my flak jacket on in Somalia. I still question my sanity over my failure to dress myself in some kind of armor in Snoul.

For the uninformed I will explain that Somalia lies in the eastern-most part of Africa. It is bordered by Djibouti to the northwest, Kenya to the southwest, the Gulf of Aden with Yemen to the north, the Indian Ocean to the east, and Ethiopia to the west. It has the longest coastline on the continent, and its terrain consists mainly of plateaus, plains and highlands. Hot conditions prevail year-round, along with periodic monsoon winds and irregular rainfall.

In 1993, the United States and the United Nations embarked on a new kind of quasi-military operation in Somalia, for which, it quickly turned out, there was no blueprint. The Clinton administration agreed for the first time to permit the American military to serve within the structure of a United Nations peacekeeping operation. Somalia began as a humanitarian mission in which troops oversaw the distribution of food—successfully, by most accounts—then suddenly became a military adventure when warlords killed a group of Pakistani soldiers.

On October 3, 1993, Somali militia fighters shot down two U.S. Black Hawk helicopters during Operation Gothic Serpent. The American assault force was out to capture the leaders of the Habr Gidr clan, headed by warlord Mohamed Farrah Aidid. The movie *Blackhawk Down* was tone perfect. It portrayed graphically just how horribly wrong the mission went.

Task Force Ranger had been organized with parts of the U.S. Army Delta Force, Ranger teams, an air element provided by the 160th Special Operations Aviation Regiment, four warriors from SEAL Team Six and members of the Air Force ParaRescue Combat Controllers. In all, it was a 160-man team. They were to go into the heart of hostile Mogadishu to bring in Aidid and the other clan leaders. The plan to arrest Aidid required the combined troops to travel from their compound on the outskirts of Mogadishu into the center of the city, which was made up of a warren of streets with which they were unfamiliar and with no maps, should they get lost.

They went in with no tanks or other armored vehicles because the Pentagon refused to supply the heavy duty armament that might have saved their lives. In spite of a direct request for armor by U.S. Forces Somalia Commander Major General Thomas M. Montgomery, Secretary of Defense Les Aspin refused. Aspin disapproved the appeal for fear of escalating the already bitter conflict between Aidid's militia and US/UN operations.

A Somali mob with thousands of combatants overran elements of the small force. Eighteen American soldiers were killed and 73 wounded. Among the images I used in my report for the *NBC Nightly News* that night was the picture of a dead American Army Ranger being dragged through the streets. Top brass at the Pentagon and elsewhere came down hard on me for transmitting the scene that lasted but a couple of seconds during the totality of the two-minute on-air story. Despite its brevity, the abrupt sight of the soldier's maltreatment illustrated vividly the utter defeat the American military had suffered.

The very public military disaster so humiliated the Pentagon and the White House that the president was expected to act. From the moment I broke the story on NBC, scooping my colleagues at CBS, ABC and CNN, and through a series of reports on the debacle in its aftermath, Aspin's time was up. He had already alienated his commanders by treating them disgracefully and showing up disorganized. Meetings he had with the generals were messy and out of sync with the highly structured methodology that governed the military's top echelon.

Aspin also was caught in the middle of the debate between President Clinton and the generals over the issue of homosexuals serving in the military. The generals, including the Chairman of the Joint Chiefs of Staff, Colin Powell, opposed gays serving openly for fear they would upset the delicate "cohesiveness" the force required.

On December 15, 1993, two months after the Somalia catastrophe, President Clinton announced Aspin's resignation for personal reasons. Given the problems Aspin encountered during his short term, most obviously the losses in Mogadishu, observers assumed the president had asked him to step down. Speculation in the media centered on the Somalia embarrassment and on Aspin's differences with the Office of Management and Budget over how much the defense budget should be cut. The secretary's cardiovascular problems, of course, also may well have been a factor.

One news magazine, the name of it long forgotten, stated that Aspin's major handicap was his politician's instinct for the middle ground on defense issues. Moreover, he seemed able to discipline neither himself nor the Pentagon bureaucracy. Aspin continued to serve as Secretary of Defense until February 3, 1994, when William J. Perry took office.

The 17-hour battle in Mogadishu was the most violent U.S. combat firefight since the Vietnam War. Three days after it ended, President Clinton cut his losses, ordering a total U.S. troop withdrawal, which occurred on March 25, 1994. Aidid was never captured. The "Black Hawk Down" incident was a mini-Vietnam, with its very own never-again lesson: no "mission creep." The Powell Doctrine was at play here with its "If you can't go in big, with all guns blazing, don't go in at all" premise adopted as gospel by many of the Pentagon's leadership.

General John Shalikashvili, or "Shali" as friends called him, had been picked by President Clinton to be Chairman of the Joint Chiefs of Staff on August 11, 1993, a little less than two months before the Blackhawk shoot down. He succeeded General Powell as the armed forces' top officer and the senior adviser to the White House on military affairs. By the time General Shalikashvili was sworn in, operations such as the humanitarian action in Somalia to save perhaps 250,000 Somalis from famine were termed as "military operations other than war," or "mootwa." Shalikashvili was said to have declared, "Real men don't do mootwa." (Shalikashvili said he was, himself, pro-mootwa, attributing the sentiment to other senior officers.)

The Clinton administration was, in fact, deeply divided over the merits of peacekeeping, with the State Department typically on one side and the Pentagon on the other. The military itself was divided on the subject, in part along generational lines. Many younger military officials came to feel peacekeeping and the inevitable political and diplomatic tasks that went with it were not a distraction from the real work, but were the real work itself, or much of it. This generation included Marine Corps leaders like General Anthony Zinni—who served as an officer or a diplomat in Kurdistan and in Somalia (where he was police chief of Mogadishu, Eritrea and the former Soviet republics)—as well as top Army figures like Wesley Clark and the former commanders in Iraq, Tommy Franks and John Abizaid.

From February 26 to March 4, 1995, I was part of the pool of war correspondents who went into Mogadishu with General Zinni and his Marines. The dangerous mission was to safeguard United Nations peacekeepers as they loaded up and left the embattled and starving Somalis to sort things out for themselves. General Shalikashvili summed up the feelings of many administration officials toward the Somalis and the continuing chaos in their capital: "They're on their own now."

It was a rapid retreat without the usual ceremonial flag-lowering. What began as a mission of mercy reached its bittersweet end, having collapsed under a combination of idealistic assumptions, an ill-conceived expansion of the mission and fatal confusions over troop command. The final pullout of the UN and U.S. Marines almost ended in yet another calamity. A high price already had been paid: the lives of 44 American soldiers, 100 other peacekeepers and hundreds of Somalis.

Somali militias watched and waited with their machineguns and other weaponry as the UN troops and their tanks retreated to awaiting ships. The final withdrawal was under cover of darkness. The heavily armed Marines put the Somali militiamen in their crosshairs. General Zinni would be the last to leave the beach in one of the AAV7-A1 Armored Amphibious Assault Vehicles that would carry him and the last of the Marines to the mother ship awaiting them just offshore in the Indian Ocean.

I and the other members of the pool waited on the beach for our ride, an armored hovercraft that skims across land and water on air cushions. Just as the LCAC came ashore, heavy bursts of lead, rocket-propelled grenades, and other shelling erupted just over our heads between the Marines and the Somali gunmen who gave us a fiery sendoff. Tracers lit up the night sky as we ran for our escape vehicle. As we boarded, we saw General Zinni jump into one of the AAV7-A1s to head out to sea, his Marines blasting away at the menacing Somalis. Later we learned that among our adversaries were operatives in al-Qaida, the same treacherous group that would claim responsibility for the attacks on America on 9/11.

The journalism pool was supposed to board the mother ship in time to cover General Zinni's arrival on board. But minutes turned to hours while our hovercraft did crazy eights on the Indian Ocean. As General Zinni's assault craft beat a hasty retreat, its engine quit. It lay motionless just a few hundred yards offshore. The general was within minutes of drowning or being killed or captured by the Somalis, as his vehicle floated back toward shore.

The mother ship lost all interest in retrieving us news people. The general had to be rescued or heads would roll, including possibly Zinni's own. Boats sent out by the mother ship and other vehicles accompanying Zinni raced toward his floundering craft. Just in time, Zinni was saved. Everybody got out without a scratch. But the clumsy ending of the evacuation mission mimicked the overall mishandling of the two-year-long peacekeeping undertaking as a whole.

Much later, General Zinni testified before the Senate Foreign Relations Committee about the colossal problems encountered during post combat stabilizations in places like Somalia and Iraq. He angrily held Pentagon officials responsible: "What is remarkable to me," he swore, "is that they have failed the president, and no one is held accountable."

24
Holding out for Some Sweet Cookies

I ought to join a club, and beat you over the head with it.
—Groucho Marx practicing literary ambiguity

America's insolence, of course, was not limited to the Far East and Africa. The U.S. is bloody cheeky all over the world. Not that Americans think of themselves as being impudent in foreign affairs. It's just that we have saddled ourselves with being the global policeman. And we may never dispel ourselves of our fundamental notion that God gave us the holy mission to spread freedom and democracy everywhere. How does the Marine hymn go?

> *From the Halls of Montezuma*
> *To the shores of Tripoli*
> *We fight our country's battles*
> *In the air, on land, and sea;*
> *First to fight for right and freedom*
> *And to keep our honor clean;*
> *We are proud to claim the title*
> *Of United States Marine.*

Specifically, I watched as we fought our country's battles in Iraq, Vietnam, Cambodia, Laos, Somalia and from many other locations including Israel and Iran.

Iran's Revolutionary Guards were my escort in 1987—the first time I traveled to the country we sometimes call Persia. The RGs are the same chaps allegedly responsible for the plot to assassinate the Saudi ambassador to the United States in 2011. They were the ones who stormed the

American Embassy in Tehran in 1979 and took 44 Americans hostage.

The RGs I knew carried AK-47 automatic machine guns strapped to their shoulders. I always watched for one of them to whirl around and shoot me, without hesitation, if I stepped out of line. I arrived in Iran at the government's invitation to witness the aftermath of a successful Iranian battle against an Iraqi outpost on the Iran-Iraq border.

Saddam Hussein had fired scud missiles topped off with deadly chemicals—weapons of mass destruction—into the midst of Iran's citizens. One hundred thousand Iranian soldiers became victims of Saddam Hussein's chemical weapons during the eight-year war with Iraq I witnessed. Innocent civilians, on both sides, had been killed. And more died every day. The scene was ghastly. Iraqi helicopters were broken and strewn across a snow-capped mountaintop overlooking the Iraqi oil hub of Kerkuk in the semiautonomous Kurdistan. Iranian gunners had shot down the choppers whose crew members were slaughtered as they tried to escape. My escorts kicked at the bodies and cursed the hated Iraqis.

Not in all my years covering combat from the blood-spattered rice paddies of Vietnam to the gruesome battlegrounds of Nicaragua had I encountered such loathing. Was there nothing at which these thugs would stop?

We did stop—my ruthless escorts and I—in the northern Iranian city of Tabriz, known for its delicious cookies. The guards jumped from their jeeps. *Uh, oh, this is where they put me up against a wall and shoot me, just for being an American.*

"You want cookies?" a guard asked, smiling. Huh? My puzzled face responded. "You want cookies? We buy cookies now," the guard said, his smile spreading ear to ear. Uh, sure, why not?

Off they went, their machine guns flopping side-to-side. And when they came back the mean men were carrying stacks of white boxes tied with pretty pink ribbons. Each of the boxes contained the yummiest cookies I'd ever tasted— plump, sugarcoated medallions filled with velvety cream stuffing that melted in my mouth. Girlfriends and boyfriends and families, too, would be the beneficiaries of the day's sweet purchases.

What a pleasant fiction this is. In a world informed by violence, how can this be? The contradictions have plagued me all the days of my life. Ambiguity is not my cup of tea. Black and white outcomes suit me well, especially for the one-minute, twenty-second spot the network requires of me. Television is such a thin medium, solitarily trying to grapple complex issues so important to viewers and doing a bad job of it. When I told the cookie story to a Marine friend of mine, he simply said, "Well, you see, even the bad guys can have a sweet tooth."

When television news switches its attentions from unspeakable evil or unspeakable good to moral shadings that shift like afternoon shadows, it has trouble. The one-minute spot will get you nowhere. And no one can be expected or should be expected to tell the truth, the whole truth and nothing but the truth on television. The bosses won't let you. Or you can't for lack of time. It is a pleasant fiction.

I went to Iran, in part, because religious Iran is a thorn in our pride. My reports were limited by Iranian censorship. Still, as limited as my reports were, some information out of

Iran was better than no information. Never mind Iraq. Never mind Afghanistan. Never mind Syria. Never mind Cuba. Never mind China, for now. We must contend with Iran. The Iranians gained overpowering influence in Iraq even as hundreds of thousands of American troops occupied that country. From the oil center in the northern city of Kerkuk to the vast oil fields at Basra in the south, Iranians occupy truly important positions of influence. The world ignores Iran at its peril. It may be a dictatorial theocracy, but it is also a formidable religious state populated by well-educated, highly skilled people prepared for anything that confronts them.

For example, the Iranian general who briefed me on his protracted war with Iraq was no tin pot dictator. He was a polished, suave man who spoke at least five languages fluently. His tactics put off the Iraqi adversaries. That Saddam Hussein was such a blundering, imprudent commander-in-chief of the Iraqi army did not go unobserved by the general. Back then the United States was at odds over what to do in the Middle East. That did not go unnoticed, either, by the general and his superiors who rule in the quasi theocratic, strong-man government. As I realized in my official and unofficial visits, Iran is unpredictable. It is a complex, experienced, modernized country whose women are not always humiliated by medieval miscreants.

The assessment of Iran is not mine alone. Heaven forbid. Don't accept my word for it. Way back in the decade of the '90s when I was visiting Iran off and on, I knew the Pentagon knew Iran was the real target in the Middle East. As the national security correspondent for NBC at the Pentagon, I was informed by officials, on background—not to be told to the public—the U.S. would invade Iraq to contain Iran. It was just a matter of time. Even before Bush-

146

the-younger was elected, his powerful neo-con advisors had the invasion plan all worked out.

Sure enough, the U.S. marched into Iraq using loose nukes as the excuse. Colin Powell told the U.N. the U.S. was duty bound to invade to safeguard weapons of mass destruction. There were no weapons of mass destruction. U.S. intelligence officers knew that all along. Saddam had gotten rid of most WMD. During and after the 2003 invasion called Operation Iraqi Freedom, invading forces did not find any stockpiles. But persistent ambiguity promoted by the Bush administration had been the cover used to attack. The U.S. didn't have to work very hard to demonize Saddam as the bogeyman with WMD, a perfect *raison d'être* to invade his country. Payback for 9/11 was the icing on the invasion. The pretext was in place.

Later, too late, we would learn there was no proof of a connection between Iraq and the terrorists who hijacked planes and attacked America. Saddam was exposed, wrongly, for cozying up to them, a great untruth, and a mammoth lie. By the time the U.S. tasked itself with peacekeeping in Iraq after the highly successful military takedown of Saddam, the Pentagon still had not gotten the conduct of post-war conciliation down pat. For the commanders, the lesson of Somalia was that this time, "Let's get it right." But they didn't. Their mistake was failure to plan for post-war Iraq in the meticulous fashion they ran the military invasion to oust Saddam. If they had thought carefully about how to occupy Iraq, far more Iraqis might have thought America had their well-being at heart. Many of the Americans who died in Iraq might have been saved if Iraqis had been led effectively to cooperate.

The Iraq war lasted eight years and nine months, cost taxpayers $800 billion and resulted in the deaths of nearly 4,500 Americans and well more than 100,000 Iraqis. With each day following U.S. pullout from Iraq, the folly of war's aftermath becomes clearer and clearer. As many expert onlookers of the Middle East have observed, Iraq's postwar order should not have been left to hazard.

Once the Bush administration's justification for war in Iraq shifted from decapitating a regime that threatened U.S. security with WMD to nurturing political transformation—first in Iraq, then throughout the Middle East—the enormous quandary that nation-building presents became authentic. The reasoning displayed by first the Bush administration and then by Obama that the U.S. could leave Iraq in good shape is intellectually impoverished and morally bankrupt. Insisting on transferring sovereignty to Iraq in 2011 while Iraqi institutions were so frail and deadly violence and chaos still raged may be regretted by the U.S. The tedious work of nation-building, once established, cannot be abandoned prematurely. To do so leaves the impression that domestic politics, pandering to anti-war fervor, make a mockery of all those Americans who sacrificed their lives for nothing.

25
New Assignment: Baghdad

I tell you folks, all politics is applesauce.
—Will Rogers, The Illiterate Digest

I jumped into the middle of the post-war muddle just after the U.S. military captured Baghdad in April 2003. Taking on a new identity, I went to work for the U.S. government in Baghdad to transform Saddam's old propaganda television network. The idea was to hire anti-Saddam Iraqis who would become truth givers just like Walter Cronkite. But in seeking and airing the truth, Walter Cronkite never had to cope with an internal battle of dual personality. Cronkite was never confronted with being a Shiite and a Sunni simultaneously. He was never at war with himself as were the Muslims who constituted Iraq. Cronkite was totally composed when seeking clarity.

Post Saddam Iraq, on the other hand, was a house divided. And the people I tried to train to pass on perspicuity reflected that division in no uncertain terms. Their world view was learned from their own ancient worlds established at birth. They had been fighting one-another for centuries. Saddam had kept them from tearing each other apart. Now, with Saddam gone, it was up to me to try to maintain order on one level. By revealing to them the magic of the First Amendment, I was supposed to fashion a happy collaboration that would belie their long time intransigence with each other. How naïve could I and my government brethren have been?

Overnight I was supposed to convince my Iraqi students to embrace the concept of the magnificence of objectivity. I was expected to wipe out their basic ignorance that denied them access to the benefits of a free press. No amount of tutoring them with U.S. media codes of ethics and responsibility could awaken in them the value of impartiality we Americans simply take for granted. A wasteland of propaganda that reinforced their subjective lives had done its job on them quite well. Generations of retraining would be required before Iraqis would be ready for *60 Minutes.* The notion that you should give your adversary a break—the proposal of fair play—would not click in their minds for years to come.

In the meantime, they would simply have to take my word for it. Good, unbiased journalism would be the gold standard of our new television network. I simply rejected scripts filled with self-serving claptrap. I cautioned them about gotcha reporting aimed at destroying each other. They would not be permitted to repeat in the newsroom their age old religious conflicts and tribal divisions. They did not like it, but I made some headway.

Just when I thought I might be on the cusp of peace and tranquility in Iraq, bolts of lightning hit my 18-story hotel in Baghdad. At least that's what I thought when at about 6 a.m. on October 26, 2003, I was shaken from slumber by immense thunder. Was this a cloudburst? Nope, it was an attack.

Twenty-eight 68mm and 85mm Katyusha rockets were fired at and struck the hotel, killing Lieutenant Colonel Charles H. Buehring and injuring 17 others. An additional 12 rockets failed to fire and remained in their tubes in the improvised launcher located less than 250 meters from the hotel. Deputy Defense Secretary Paul Wolfowitz was staying in the hotel the night of the attack but was unhurt, while author and Department of Labor official Craig Davis was injured.

Now, a decade on, the U.S. is indebted to war for $1 trillion and indebted to the families of 4,500 Americans who gave their lives in Iraq and to 30,000 others who were wounded. And perhaps the supreme insult is this: The devious plan to keep Iran in check failed miserably. The U.S. is scrambling to prevent Iran from realizing its ambition to dominate the Middle East. Both Israel and the United States realize stopping the Iranian powerhouse in its pursuit of nuclear weapons is no simple military invasion or drone bombing. Israel stopped Iraq from going nuclear way back in 1981 by bombing its atomic plant, located out in the open, 18 miles south of Baghdad.

Fearing another Israeli air attack, Iran put its plant deep underground to frustrate the Israeli Air Force. But Iran's nuclear scientists are not off limits. Taking them out, though, and infecting their nuclear processes with computer viruses won't get it. That is the reason the United States has been building newly invented bunker-busting bombs weighing 30,000 pounds each. The bombs can penetrate Iran's underground nuclear plant even if the atomic installations are 200 feet down. So, now, the United States is trying to build a pretext for going to war in Iran just as it constructed the lie to attack Iraq. The U.S. and its Arab friends are planning to hit Iran with everything they have, leaving Israel in the wings with plausible deniability.

I watched from my listening post inside Iran as the United States conducted its devastating aerial attacks on Iraq at the outset of the first Gulf War. The outcome of that war was never in doubt. Coalition forces rounded up by President George Bush the elder, and led by America, doomed Saddam Hussein from the outset. Those same forces will be in even greater demand today if the U.S. goes into Iran. The Iraqis under Saddam were as zilch compared to the Iranians. Saddam tried to save his air force by ordering his pilots to fly their fighter and bomber aircraft to neighboring Iran. The Iranians smiled, welcomed the planes and never returned any of them to Saddam. And every time an Iraqi tank was blasted in the U.S.-led war, the Iranians privately cheered.

Yet, some Iranians told me they were being stymied by their leaders. They wanted an end to the authoritarian regime run by scoundrels increasingly bent on preserving religious intolerance. They wanted a government that would be more representative of and responsive to their needs. The Iranian employees at Iran's TV facilities told me they were limited by their superiors, who were hard core religionists. They admired our advancements in television and internet communications, which they wanted to emulate. They hoped to adopt Western advancement in broadcast technologies. But every time they tried, the Iranians told me, they were stopped and punished by the mullahs who run things at Iran TV. The religionists relentlessly crushed any opposition. Increasingly timid, challengers of the powerful regime had almost given up.

Consequently the U.S. came to the conclusion that simply supporting the opposition in Iran will not be enough to change the government and oust its leaders. Nor will sanctions. There is not enough time left. Iran is close, very close to carrying out its aim to be a nuclear power. Once done, it will use its missiles tipped with atomic bombs to threaten Israel, other Middle East countries, Europe and the United States.

A collective unequivocal assault by coalition forces using conventional military forces and special operations groups combined with non-traditional methodology may be in the offing. In other words, government experts not authorized to speak publicly on the subject tell me the U.S. has plans to decapitate the current Iranian leadership and destroy Iran's nuclear potential by hitting hard with its military and non-military power. But the pretext to do so must be set.

Remember the story about how the Iranians were planning to kill the Saudi ambassador on American soil? In the interim, both Israel and the United States are using cyber warfare such as computer viruses to interrupt Iran's nuclear program. But high-tech drones, viruses and air strikes will not defeat the Iranian regime, according to military sources. Only a war with boots on the ground has a chance.

IV
Tin-Horn Dictators and Other Scalawags

26
Noriega

Could this be the <u>beginning</u> of a beautiful friendship?
—Paraphrase from *Casablanca* (with apologies to
Humphrey Bogart)

When it comes to the superciliousness with which a country struts when going to war, America has no competitor. Nowhere is that more true than in Latin America, another one of my beats. Before Vietnam came along, America pretty much had had its own way. With the CIA in the lead, the U.S. was incredibly successful, especially in the Western Hemisphere. We carried a big stick down there, swaggering to enforce the Monroe Doctrine.

In Chile it was the CIA-orchestrated overthrow and assassination of Salvador Allende. He was a Chilean physician and politician generally considered the first democratically elected Marxist to become president of a country in Latin America. General Augusto Pinochet took over and became the latest strong-man in America's holster of military dictators. He came at a high price, but America could afford to buy his friendship to help keep the Soviets and Communism out of our backyard.

In Nicaragua we embraced the dictator General Anastasio Somoza, buying some more friendship. In Guatemala we used our CIA to oust Jacobo Arbenz Guzman. A suspected crypto-communist, Arbenz was Guatemala's democratically elected president who instituted land reform, thus threatening the vast holdings of U.S. companies like United Fruit. After the CIA bombed his place in Guatemala City,

Arbenz was replaced by military dictators with whom we were cozy and became fast friends.

It's difficult to believe the number of Latin tyrants we created and supported. Fidel Castro is the only one of them who is a thorn in our pride to this day. The CIA could not control or kill him no matter how hard it tried. In fact, Castro humiliated the CIA. Puffed up by its earlier, astounding successes, the CIA figured it could easily overthrow Castro at the Bay of Pigs. It figured wrong. I'll share more about the fiasco at the Bahia de Cochinos later.

In Panama, Washington's old friend and CIA spy-master, military dictator General Manuel Noriega, served America's purposes up to a point. He allowed the U.S. to set up listening posts in Panama. He aided the American-backed Contra guerrillas in Nicaragua by acting as a conduit for U.S. money and weapons. U.S. prosecutors of Noriega said the CIA and the U.S. military paid Noriega about $360,000. Noriega claims the payment was more in the range of $10,000,000.

Whatever the case, in 1984, Noriega went off the reservation. He rebuffed demands by U.S. Marine Corps Lieutenant Colonel Oliver North that he provide military assistance to the Nicaraguan Contras. North was a National Security Council operative later charged with criminal wrongdoing in the infamous Iran-Contra affair. In May 1989, "the dictator," as former President Jimmy Carter labeled him, "stole the election." Our cameras and I were covering the presidential election when voting observer Carter, his carotid arteries pulsating, denounced Noriega for rigging the vote. The opposition, he pronounced, had really won; the U.S. recognized Guillermo Endara as the new president.

The day following that announcement Endara, along with vice-presidential candidates Ricardo Arias Calderón and Guillermo Ford, rolled through the old part of the Panamanian capital in a triumphant motorcade. They were intercepted by a detachment of Noriega's paramilitary ruffians called Dignity Battalions. A couple of troops protected Arias Calderón, but Endara and Ford were badly beaten. Images of Ford running to safety with his Guayabera shirt covered in blood were broadcast by us in the United States and around the world.

On December 20, 1989, the United States launched a military invasion to capture Noriega and bring him to justice. President George H.W. Bush justified the invasion, citing the killing of a U.S. serviceman by some of Noriega's troops at a checkpoint. On the eve of the invasion I took my camera crew to Noriega's command headquarters, where the Dignity Battalion thugs were being armed with AK-47 assault machine guns. Noriega's national guardsmen were on high alert. Noriega's men manned anti-aircraft guns.

United States troops, already in country to protect the Panama Canal, were at battle stations. U.S. military aircraft, mostly C-130s and C-141s arrived at Howard Air Force base located within the zone. It looked like an invasion was imminent, but nobody would confirm it was coming down that night.

In Washington, Joint Chiefs Chairman Colin Powell watched my report on *NBC Nightly News.* He knew elements of the 82nd Airborne Division were about to parachute into the Panama City International Airport. More than 27,000 American soldiers, the largest U.S. invasion force since Vietnam, were on the verge of entering Panama by force. Powell, of course, was concerned I might report something that would jeopardize the invading forces. Here's part of what I reported that night:

Rabel: United States C-141 Starlifters flew
        into Panama this afternoon, one
        landing every ten minutes. At the same
        time these aircraft were arriving,
        security was tightened around the
        airbase. U.S. soldiers could be seen in
        full combat gear on roads around the
        base. No one here could confirm that
        these aircraft were part of a U.S.
        invasion group. But tensions on both
        sides are high this evening over the
        possibility of a U.S. strike.

Powell breathed a sigh of relief. In his book, *The
Commanders,* Bob Woodward writes that Powell was
relieved I had not jumped the gun. Woodward wrote that
Powell thought, "Mighty close but no compromise." Powell
realized he would wind up having to thank some reporters.
I'm still waiting for the thank you call. (Just kidding.)

Apparently Noriega did not think the U.S. would invade. I
am told he was at his girlfriend's house when the
parachutes began to fall. Eastern Airlines had just landed
the final commercial flight of the evening. The flight crew
was on the way to the hotel where I was staying, the
Marriott. I was on the top floor in my room when the first
bombs slammed into Noriega's headquarters. A lot of the
action could be seen from my window.

F-117 Nighthawk stealth fighters streaked in for the first
time in combat. Navy SEAL teams—like the one that killed
Osama bin Laden and the one that rescued an American
aid worker and her Danish colleague from Somali pirates—
were ordered to hit three targets: Panamanian Defense
Forces in Balboa Harbor, PDF assets on Flamenco Island,
and Noriega's private jet at Paitilla Airport, which was within

walking distance of the Marriott. Almost immediately upon landing, the 48-man special operations team came under withering fire from the PDF guarding Noriega's plane. Although Noriega's jet was eventually destroyed, the SEALs suffered four dead and 13 wounded.

Before I could get out of the hotel to join my camera crew in the fighting, Dignity Battalion paramilitary goons had surrounded the building. They went room-to-room, breaking down doors and taking guests hostage. I was on the phone with NBC in New York broadcasting live on the air. With lights out, I spoke in a low voice to not be overheard by the goons outside my door. They slammed the butts of their AK-47s against the door, but it held. Next door they caught and detained my editor and took her down to the ground floor where she was thrown in with all the other guests who had been rounded up.

I continued broadcasting throughout the night and into the morning. On NBC's *Today* broadcast, Bryant Gumbel and Jane Pauley and I went over every aspect of the assault, which had been a success, except that Noriega was still at large. And so were many of the Ding Bats, the new name for the Dignity Battalions. They were still menacing the hotel, but they had begun to drift out of sight as 82nd Airborne Rangers took control of the city.

Throughout the Canal Zone, the *Today* show could be heard via the Armed Forces Radio and Television Service, or A-farts as it was commonly known. The Ding Bats could hear everything Bryant, Jane and I were saying. So when Bryant asked me to divulge my exact whereabouts, I was sort of at a loss. If I told him I was in the hotel, I would be giving away my location to the enemy.

There was a place to take refuge in the basement of the hotel. Marriott employees did their best to hide the guests who'd escaped the paramilitary hoodlums. I joined them, taking up residence behind a water tank in the laundry room. A British diplomat, his wife and newborn baby were among the other guests. The crying baby needed warm milk in a baby bottle. Mom and dad were frightened for their lives. Trying to cheer them up by distracting them, I asked about their diplomatic responsibilities, and why they had just arrived in Panama. "For safety," the Brit said. "To get away from the drug violence surrounding my diplomatic post in Colombia, I asked for a transfer to a more quiet and peaceful setting. So London sent me here." He didn't say, "Go figure." We didn't talk that way back then. What he probably said—I couldn't quite hear him—was something like, "Aww, shit."

I escaped from the hotel with my editor in tow and fled to a safe house the camera crew had set up for us. The editor had been released by her captors, as had all the others who had been taken. The Ding Bats had thought they could use their captives as ransom for the release of Noriega, but he was still in hiding. And the leaderless paramilitary units were on the run from the advancing 82nd Airborne troops.

The city was in chaos, still, with some of the PDF and paramilitary groups in firefights with the American soldiers. I managed to leave the safe house to uplink the combat story my camera crew and I had produced, and then headed back to the hotel to fetch our belongings. A lot of the shooting was occurring around the hotel. We hadn't quite made it to the hotel when shots rang out. Gunfire hit and killed two news people on the other side of the hotel, catching them in crossfire between friendly American forces. As I climbed an embankment to enter the hotel, a trooper from the 82nd wheeled around and stopped just short of pulling the trigger. He herded me into a Marriott truck, where I was almost trampled to death by hotel guests and employees fleeing the barrage of bullets.

160

The truck sped through some neighborhoods, taking fire from all sides. There were some hits, but we managed to get to waiting U.S. helicopters on the beach. We flew to Howard Air Force base in the Canal Zone. And I headed back to Washington.

On *Meet the Press,* Tim Russert and I were in search of Noriega, who had managed to avoid capture. One of Noriega's options, I told Russert, was to hide out in Panama's jungles. However, Noriega opted to take refuge in the Vatican Embassy in the middle of the city. Exhausted and tormented by deafening heavy metal music that psyops (psychological operations) troops directed at the Vatican Embassy, Noriega surrendered on Jan. 4, 1990. He was convicted on drug and racketeering charges in 1992 and, at the conclusion of his prison sentence, was extradited to France in 2010. He served additional time in France for money laundering.

France extradited him to Panama, and on December 11, 2011, Noriega, 77, arrived at El Renacer Prison, a former American facility in Panama, to complete a 20-year sentence for three convictions stemming from several deaths and await further judgment in Panama's courts. His foes in Panama, who call him Pineapple Face, a reference to Noriega's severe acne and resulting scars, wish to see him die in prison. They also wish his return to Panama will remind people democracy should not be taken for granted. They may get their wishes.

27
Fred Sherwood

...in the Western Hemisphere the adherence
of the United States to the Monroe Doctrine
may force the United States...to the exercise
of an international police power.
—Theodore Roosevelt,
The Roosevelt Corollary to the Monroe Doctrine (1905)

In Guatemala the CIA supported right wing governments
that were in power when 200,000 citizens died in savage
bloodletting. According to The Historical Clarification
Commission, an independent human rights body, the
Guatemalan army was responsible for 93 percent of the
killings that occurred in the 1980s. Leftist guerrillas
murdered three percent, and four percent were listed as
unresolved. The HCC report documented that in the 1980s,
the army committed 626 massacres against Mayan
[indigenous] villages. "The massacres that eliminated entire
Mayan villages are neither perfidious allegations nor
figments of the imagination, but an authentic chapter in
Guatemala's history," the commission concluded.

What is more, the report said the U.S. Government and the
CIA provided direct and in direct support for some
Guatemalan military operations which included, but were
not limited to: "...acts of genocide" against the Mayans.
The report found that Guatemalan army soldiers routinely
"...raped and tortured women, then murdered them...a
common practice."

President Bill Clinton apologized for the past U.S. support
of right-wing regimes in Guatemala. On March 10, 1999,

Clinton visited Central America and announced: "For the United States, it is important that I state clearly that support for military forces and intelligence units which engaged in violence and widespread repression was wrong, and the United States must not repeat that mistake."

Make no mistake. The U.S. supported those atrocities. When I went to Guatemala in 1982 to do an hour-long documentary on the savagery for *CBS Reports*, I found a former American pilot, Fred Sherwood, who had flown CIA missions to help overthrow the democratically elected president, Jacobo Arbenz Guzman. Fred Sherwood took no pains to hide his approval of state terrorism in the service of Guatemalan business interests, including some 200 U.S. corporations. Sherwood himself owned a rubber plantation, a cement factory and a textile mill, where he paid his workers about $4.50 a day.

I interviewed him on-camera at his luxurious Guatemala City home, where he had taken up residency and was living the good life.

> Rabel: The whole country of Guatemala was once virtually a branch office of the United Fruit Company. In the 1950s,it held two-thirds of the usable farmland and monopolized the nation's railroads in its multimillion-dollar banana empire. When a democratically elected president named Jacobo Arbenz tried to institute a land reform program in1954 so poor farmers could have land of their own, United Fruit lobbied the Eisenhower administration to intervene. The CIA stepped in and overthrew the Guatemalan leader ... [Sherwood says] it's an ideal place to

invest...because profits are high, costs are low.

Sherwood: We have a huge labor market, and the workers are very good. You teach them and the ... they don't mind doing the same thing day after day, the routine, like American workers like a variation. But here, people do the same thing day after day, and they're very good.

Rabel: Is the government pretty cooperative?

Sherwood: Oh, yes. They're very cooperative. We don't have restrictions as to environmental things and there's just no restrictions or rules at all, so that makes it nice.

Rabel: Are the people here oppressed in any way?

Sherwood: Really, I don't think so. I know of no individual, I know of no one—I have lived here for 36 years, I've been in farming, in industry, in commerce—and I don't know of anybody being impressed [sic]. No one forces them to do anything. And I think this is just something some reporters have thought up.

Rabel: Most Guatemalans see a different country than Fred Sherwood does. Human rights organizations have repeatedly accused Guatemalan

164

governments of running deliberate programs of political murder to maintain a grip on power—priests, nuns, labor leaders, teachers, students—anyone who threatened the established order. Politicians have always been high on the hit list. A [Christian Democrat] politician here in this country told me that more than 120 of his party's leaders had been assassinated in about an 18-month period.

Sherwood: Well, in the first place, I'd very much question it, because I don't think there's been a hundred twenty people of all types assassinated here in the last year. I mean, I'm not counting the peasants or the—I mean men of that category. No, I think that's probably exaggerated to a great extent. There were a couple of politicians assassinated a few years ago, but believe me, they were way out in left field and well, these people are, I think, our enemies. They're … they against our… our way of life. And maybe assassination is not the right word for it, but I don't think they should be … continue allowed to run free to try to destroy our form of government, our way of life in other words.

Did I hear Sherwood say the 200,000 Guatemalans murdered by the CIA backed army was "…just something that some reporters thought up"? I mean, I could rewind and play the interview for you. Listen, please. We couldn't have thought up Fred Sherwood if we had tried.

28
Pinochet

I am not a dictator. It's just that I have a grumpy face.
–Augusto Pinochet

As the U.S. proudly marketed its democracy and respect for human rights in its worldwide battle against Communism, it used every anti-democratic tool it could find to combat the foe. The legacy of human rights abuses by the U.S. in its struggle to defeat Moscow is legendary. It taught dictators how to kill leftists, and in so doing promoted the murder of innocent civilians. It instructed despots on how to set up death squads, and then turned a blind eye as rape and torture and murder were carried out.

Perhaps there is no place better than Chile to illustrate the dreadful tactics the CIA used to intimidate and wipe out assumed opponents. Henry Kissinger said, "I don't see why we need to stand by and see a country go Communist due to the irresponsibility of its own people." He was talking about the fact Chileans had freely, not irresponsibly, elected a Marxist, Salvador Allende, as president. Democracy was okay unless the wrong candidate got elected. When that happened America tossed aside its principles and went after the freedom-loving culprits with a vengeance.

This and more I pointed out on Sunday, August 18, 1983, in my *CBS Sunday Morning* report from Santiago, Chile. Chilean street scenes displaying protests and goose-stepping military were shown throughout. The abbreviated transcript:

Anchor: And so the U.S. spent several million dollars, principally through the CIA, to overturn the Allende government. Allende was finally overthrown and killed. What replaced him, some ten years ago, was a military dictatorship headed by Augusto Pinochet. But now, democratic Chileans are raising their voices again, and the dictator may be in trouble. That's our cover story, reported by Ed Rabel.

Rabel: Ten years ago, the people of Chile lost their voice; now they are finding it again. ... During nearly 150 years of democracy, the people of Chile could speak up and get away with it, just like in America. They don't get away with it much anymore. ... A military dictatorship has been running Chile for a decade, ever since General Augusto Pinochet led a coup in which Chile's last democratically elected president, the Marxist Salvador Allende, died.

Chilean poet, novelist and intellectual Ariel Dorfman: I think I just got too much used to democracy. You know, I left Chile two or three months after the coup, and I've been living in France and Holland and the United States, where it is inconceivable that somebody should come and—and kill you because of your opinions.

Rabel: Ariel Dorfman... was ordered into exile by Pinochet ten years ago, along with thousands of other citizens. Now Pinochet has permitted him and some of the other exiles to return, a concession to the opposition. The people of Chile are finding their voice again.

Dorfman: We are trying here to establish a democracy, and we are also trying to create a system which would have social justice. We tried under Allende and we failed. We're going to try again. … Here there are people who are menaced with bullets, with jail, with exile, and they're fighting in the streets; they're shouting what they think of. That's a good example of courage. It means that here are people who think more of freedom than they do of their lives.

Rabel: In America, if people don't like somebody in office, they can vote him out. In Chile, nobody but the army can get Pinochet out. And so far, he has their support. What is more, Pinochet says that a new constitution, approved in a 1980 plebiscite, gives him the right to govern for six more years, when he's promised to install what he calls a new democracy. But now, a wide spectrum of Chileans are saying they can't afford to wait any longer. … High government officials contend the president still has the support of the majority of the people. "Just look at this outpouring of support during a celebration in Santiago, marking the tenth anniversary of the coup," they tell us. ... Unemployment and under-employment are rising rapidly.

Dorfman: You've seen the ... the young kids who really have no hope of anything except just throwing a stone to somebody. That's because they have been untrained, unlearned from democracy. They have ... they do not have the channels through which they used to be able to express themselves.

Catholic priest Mariano Puga: For them, being unemployed is sort of ... how would you call that? ...would call it a crisis del hombre. Eh?

Rabel: Crisis of man.

Puga: Crisis of man. They ... they consider themselves underdeveloped man.

Rabel: In Pudahauel, a shantytown, 70 percent of the people ... are without work. Some have welfare jobs, which pay from 20 to 40 dollars a month. Malnutrition, drug abuse, alcoholism, child-beating are said to be prevalent. A third of the people of Chile are believed to live this way, and most of those people blame Pinochet.

Puga: People who ask themselves, "What's the good of living? Hmmm? What are we living for? What's the good of struggling for life, hmmm, when there's no future? What's the good of studying where there's no future? What's the good of looking for work when there's no work? What's the good of struggling for justice when we gain nothing?"

Rabel: Still, the people of Chile are finding their voice. [People singing] … The words say, "Don't oppress the poor man and the orphan. Don't deny him an income or steal his bread, pretending to help him." They are the words of protest. … The military government says those behind the protests in the shantytowns are Communists who want to return Chile to the days of Allende, the days of Marxism.

Dorfman: I think this is like the bogeyman. You … I mean, you keep on saying, "Those years are going to come back. Watch out." And those years are not going to come back.

Rabel: Heraldo Munos, educated in the United States, is a leading professor of political science at the University of Chile.

Munos: To a certain extent, one can say that Americans take their democracy for granted. … It is, I think, important to … to remind them that this is not something that is for granted. It is something that one should build and reinforce day by day, and there is something very tragic if one loses it.

Rabel: Not just the poor are feeling the loss in Chile. The problems are beginning to cut across class lines. This is Valparaiso, Chile's main port, and it is symbolic of the country's economic problems. Foreign goods pour through here under the military government's liberal import policy, which has wiped out half the country's domestic production capacity. A lot of the stuff that comes in here was made in the United States, but one thing Chile is not importing from America these days is democracy. The middle class, the backbone of Chilean society, has discovered it has completely lost its political leverage and its social identity. There are 450,000 homeowners who are trying to reschedule their mortgages, unable to keep up current payments. The national debt is estimated at $29 billion. Inflation is at about 35 percent.

Rabel: Father Gerald Whalen was born in Detroit. He has watched the political process in Chile since 1955.

Walen: It would seem to me that the ... the return to the democracy would produce a situation whereby the people would feel they have a voice. Chile is a very patient country, and that's why when they took to the streets, they took to

172

the streets only as a last measure. …
But who can justify injuring and killing
people with guns? The people you are
shooting at have no arms. And they're
your own people. You're shooting your
own … your own brothers, and that's
creating a very serious problem.

Dorfman: So, what has come here is that
we've … we've all lost our humanity,
both those who have shot the bullets
and those who have received them. I
really would invite the American people
to … to think more about us as human
beings that suffer, that have a lot of
hope. This means, of course, that you
must understand, in the States, that we
are as human as you are, and that
therefore a hungry person here is as
hungry as a person anywhere, and that
when one person dies here it's as if he
were dying there, in the United States.

Rabel: Something extraordinary happened
the other day at the funeral of Miguel
Zavala, a common man. Ten thousand
Chileans joined his funeral march
spontaneously. It was something the
authorities could not ignore.

Dorfman: This is the way democracies are …
are created. They're never created
easily. There must be suffering. It's got
to be difficult; I mean, it … it can't be
easy because we're … we're breaking
an old world. And to create a new

173

world is ... is a very difficult thing, and
a glorious thing to do.

The humanity of Chileans in 1983 is the humanity of
Americans in 2012. The suffering of the unemployed of
Chile in 1983 is the suffering by the unemployed of
America in 2012. The loss by Chilean middle class
homeowners in 1983 is the loss by America's homeless in
2012. And the hungry children of Chile in 1983 are the
same hungry children in America in 2012.

Some will say comparing America in 2012 to the
dictatorship of Chile in 1983 is a leap nobody should make,
a jump without foundation, a fabrication. Tell that to those
who have participated in the Occupy Wall Street
movement, those who have been gassed and beaten for
their trouble. Tell that to the 13 million who are
unemployed. Tell that to the ¾ of a million men, women
and children who are homeless on any given night. And tell
that to the 5 ½ million homeowners who can't pay their
mortgages. They know better.

Chile finally returned to democratic rule in 1990.

In March 1998 Pinochet resigned as head of the Chilean
army but became a senator, therefore guaranteeing him
parliamentary immunity for life. However, later that year
while on a visit to London, Pinochet was arrested by the
British police, following a request by judges investigating
the torture and disappearance of Spanish citizens during
Pinochet's period in power.

He faced extradition to Spain to face prosecution, however,
the British gave permission for Pinochet to return to Chile
on compassionate grounds. When he arrived home the
authorities in Chile stripped him of his parliamentary
immunity and proceedings against him began. Eventually,

in July 2001 the Chilean courts decided to suspend the investigation on grounds of "dementia."

In 2005 a US Senate investigation of terrorist financing discovered that Pinochet had opened and closed at least 128 bank accounts at Riggs Bank and other U.S. financial institutions in an apparent money-laundering operation. It seems that Pinochet had illegally obtained a $28 million fortune during his period as a dictator of Chile.

On Sunday, December 10, 2006, Pinochet died at the age of 91. His legacy—the death or disappearance of over 3,000 Chilean citizens and the torture of thousands more. What a pathetic ending.

29
Uncle Sam

Give me your tired, your poor,
Your huddled masses yearning to breathe free,
The wretched refuse of your teeming shore.
—Emma Lazarus, "The New Colossus"

"South of the Border, Down Mexico Way" was a popular song written by Jimmy Kennedy and Michael Carr in 1939. Patsy Cline, Gene Autry and Shep Fields recorded the song. But Frank Sinatra sang the most famous version in 1953. The source of the sadness in that melody is in Mexico. In the lyrics, a man looks south of the U.S./Mexico border with regret and pain for having lied to the woman he can't forget, having returned for her too late, just as she was preparing for marriage to another man.

In the song's lyrical information lies the analogous concept of the heart-breaking relationship the United States has with Mexico, its closest neighbor to the south. At the center of that distressing connection is the profoundly complicated matter of immigration. In the desire to curb the huge illegal exodus from Mexico, the U.S. contradicts and stains its own sterling reputation as the beacon of hope for the deprived of the world.

In the heated 2011-12 U.S. primary presidential campaign, candidates debated whether Mexicans should be electrocuted or otherwise wasted when caught trying to cross the border. Lost in the unconscionable argument is the historical imperative that the U.S. planted itself in the Southwest on Mexican land. If anything, the U.S. insinuated itself into Mexico and set itself up as a bulwark, not a receptor of the people from whom territory was taken. The arrogance of the mocking equation is obvious. Perhaps the question in the great immigration dispute ought to be how Mexico should keep Americans out of its patrimony, not the other way around.

On January 11, 1981, I looked into the vexing problem, as upsetting then as it is today. It was *Sunday Morning* on *CBS*. Much of the film showed illegal border crossings into the U.S. A shortened version of the transcript follows:

> Charles Kuralt: How do the United States and Mexico get along? Disagreeably, as usual. The United States and Mexico just do not speak the same language. Our *Sunday Morning* cover story, reported by Ed Rabel: "Mexico and Us."
>
> Ed Rabel: A Mexican ruler once said, "Poor Mexico, so far from God and so close to the United States." ... There was a time when Mexicans did not have to come here this way. This was their land—San Diego, San Francisco, Tucson, Santa Fe, places Mexicans could call home. Now they must have permission to come and work here. Without it, they are called illegal aliens. ... This family crossed the Rio Grande on an inner tube. Abandoned by their guides, they walked through snake-infested wasteland. They said they would do it repeatedly to get to America.

Arriaga, father of family: (English subtitles): I am willing to risk anything to give my family a better life. There's always a great fear that somebody will report me to the immigration service, but I'm willing to take this risk because of the better life here. I want my children to have a better education in both languages, then they will have a better opportunity.

Rabel: The people are Spanish descendants. In fact, Spanish descendants account for more than half of the city's population. It is San Antonio, the 10th largest city in the United States. It, too, was once a part of Mexico.

Historian T.R. Fehrenbach: As the Mexicans see it, we took one-third of the historic Mexican territory away from them. This is something that I don't think lies strongly in the mind of Americans. The … you know, the winners don't think of it that … quite this way. … There had been several hundred actual violations of Mexican territory or Mexican sovereignty by the United States. These are still raw wounds. They're very conscious of it. And to them, it was a humiliation; it was a sign that we did not respect them as a fully sovereign nation. … There is a definite feeling in Mexico that somehow the rise of this great, powerful English-speaking nation, this colossus of the north on the North American Continent, aborted and thwarted their history, which could have been the rise of a 200-million-strong Spanish-speaking empire.

Rabel: When you have been quarreling with your neighbors for nearly a hundred years, making up is hard to do, but last week Ronald Reagan went over to his neighbor's house to try to patch things up. This was the first meeting ever between an American President-elect and the President of Mexico. The idea that the new Reagan administration will become militarily involved in El Salvador's internal affairs is a big issue in Mexico. The rest of Latin America looks to Mexico as a leader in that part of the world. President Lopez Portillo has already warned America not to interfere. Just how much of its billions of barrels of oil Mexico will be willing to deliver to us is a big issue in the United States. Lopez Portillo says Mexico will limit its production. Because of Mexico's political and economic importance, America is paying its southern neighbor more attention than ever before. Americans want more and more of Mexico's oil to keep flowing across the border, but what many don't want crossing over are the Mexicans themselves … the hundreds of thousands who come here illegally in search of jobs.

American worker Lucky Kahler: Work's hard
enough as it is. It's hard to make a
living, without them guys coming over
here and taking it away from us. Takes
it … work away from a … a man from
the United States, from his own
country. And wages, of course, will
dri— will drop, because they work for
little or nothing.

Rabel: What do you think the government
ought to do?

Kahler: They need to stop it. It has to come
from the government to stop it. They
have to … only the legal people
working here, or leave them back
where they … let them work where
they come from. And we couldn't work
in Mexico. That … they don't allow
that.

American worker James Groesbeck: The
people over here in the United States,
they got to make a living, too, and so
why should they come back from over
across the border and then come back
in and take your job away from you?

Rabel: Mexican workers entering America
unlawfully represent the most nagging,
if not the biggest, point of conflict
between the United States and Mexico.
Some illegal aliens are currently
employed at this San Antonio salvage
yard, which has been raided several
times by immigration officials.

180

However, their employer, Alton Newell, keeps hiring them and denies that they take jobs that U.S. citizens want.

American employer Alton Newell: Let me say it truthfully, with welfare and food-stamp programs here, there are a lot of people that don't want to work. If ... if we didn't have any illegal aliens, I would say we would be short of labor, because our people are not ... are not looking for this kind of work. And like I said a while ago, with welfare and food stamps and unemployment compensation, a lot of people don't want to work.

Rabel: There is the view that America would have a tough time without the undocumented workers. There is also the view that Mexico would have even a tougher time without them.

Fehrenbach: Mexico has a ... a typical Third World economy, in the sense that it's a very poor industrial infrastructure, has very ... a very low, improvised base. It is not industrializing or creating jobs or opportunity nearly as fast as its population is rising. Consequently, they need the safety valve. They need to send some millions of their young people to work in the United States, where they not only get rid of them and their unrest at home ... Remember, 40 percent of the Mexican working population is either unemployed or underemployed. It's a figure ... it's ... it boggles the mind. If we do not help Mexico in some sense, solve this demographic time bomb, then we can absolutely destroy a ... a regime such as Lopez Portillo's, and what we would get would probably be much less to our liking.

Rabel: They are so desperate, so hungry, to come here that they are willing to risk anything, even death. Many died last year after the guides they hired to protect them from the border patrol abandoned them in the scorching desert. ... Sixteen-year-old Santiago Flores is an illegal alien from Matamoros. He says he paid some men $600 for safe passage across the border to the U.S., but that he went without food for five days during the dangerous journey. Serafin Rodriguez earns $5.75 an hour in San Antonio as a construction worker. In his Mexican hometown he could find no work. He also is here illegally.

Serafin Fodreiguez: It's better over here than in Mexico, because you can making some more money over here than Mexico, because over there you no got too much jobs. And [indistinct] got a lot of troubles over there. I need to open the ... a business over there, a big business, make you a lot of work; so over ... that's why the people come here. That's why come here not for

making any trouble, nothing like that.
That is why I come here, because I …
over there they no got too much jobs. I
want to stay here, because … and the
first thing I got my wife. And a …
another things, I don't got nothing to do
in … to Mexico. I don't like Mexico.

Rabel: Rodriguez married a United States
citizen, a Mexican-American. He hopes
to become a citizen one day. He and
his wife are starting their lives together
in America in this $60-a-month,
tumbledown house on San Antonio's
southwest side. It is, they believe, a
beginning. Franklin Roosevelt said it:
"Remember, remember always, that all
of us are descended from immigrants."
This family of illegal aliens wants to be
part of that tradition, be it legally or
illegally. And one family member
already is, legally. Rachel was born
here. She is a United States citizen—
the beginning for this family of the
realization of the American dream.

Arriaga (in Spanish with English subtitles): I
like and believe in the American
dream. I hope eventually that I will
become an American citizen, so that I
can buy my property here and live just
like anybody else.

President Obama is working on the immigration problem
despite right-wing criticism that he pampers fence jumpers.
By executive order, Mr. Obama permitted youngsters
brought in by their parents when the kids were infants to

continue in the U.S. barring any bad behavior. It is the right thing to do. The truth is, lots of restaurants in the U.S. couldn't get a dish washed if it weren't for illegal immigrants. Houses could not be built. Trenches could not be dug. Crops could not be harvested. The dirty work of America would never be done without them. Oh, and by the way, lots and lots of illegals turn out to do better in school than the native born.

30
Castro

Cuba is a walk down memory lane. It is a country whose citizens stopped counting the years in 1958. That's the year Fidel took over. Somehow a warp drive spaceship picked up 12 million people, streaked back in time and dropped them off on an island where art-deco is not out-of date. When the family goes out for a Sunday afternoon spin in Havana, they ride in '57 Chevy Bel Airs and hard tops and convertibles with anodized aluminum body panels, long-tailed rear fins, front bumper and hood birds. The cars are Detroit's "Sweet, Smooth and Sassy" productions that collectors die for and Cubans find quite pedestrian.

Gorgeous showgirls wear bananas on top of their heads at the Tropicana. Ricky Ricardo's bongo drums beat wildly in the streets while pretty, bronzed Latinas show off their dancing skills and other charms as well.

The Old Man and The Sea is alive and doing just fine in Cojimar. Hemingway's house is precisely as he left it, all his old books on the shelves guarded by huge heads of antelopes and other African beasts he shot and killed, mounted on the walls. His hunting jackets are carefully hung in the closets. And his 1921 Corona #3 typewriter is where he left it, a blank sheet of paper in it waiting to be immortalized.

Cuba is both a vocation and an avocation for me. The first time I went there, in 1975, the Cold War had frozen relations with the United States. Soviet red military brigades marched militantly alongside the Fuerzas Armadas Revolucionarias de Cuba only 90 miles from Florida.

This was a Cuba just 12 years removed from the missile crisis of 1963, which almost immolated all of humankind. Castro was in a snit, kicking the walls when Soviet Premier Khrushchev gave in to President Kennedy, removing all of his missiles. *"No cojones, no cojones!"* Castro screamed when the Soviets pulled out their rockets that were already on launch pads installed in the eastern part of the island. From there, the deadly missiles could have wiped out Washington, D.C., and several other U.S. cities, killing millions of Americans. Fortunately, Khrushchev had kept the missiles under strict Soviet control, forbidding Cubans from getting anywhere close to the missile sites. If Castro had gotten his fingers on the nuclear button, the megalomaniac would have pushed it, without doubt.

As it was, Soviet commanders on the ground in Cuba were armed with tactical nuclear weapons in addition to the strategic missiles they had agreed to vacate. They planned to use the smaller, battlefield nukes against any American military attack. Presumably, Air Force General Curtis LeMay did not know about the tactical weapons when he advised Mr. Kennedy to invade Cuba on the ground and in the air to smash the Russian offensive missiles.

Nobody else in Washington knew about the tactical weaponry, either. If President Kennedy had taken the advice of LeMay and other top U.S. brass and ordered an assault, thousands of American soldiers would have died in a mushroom cloud on Cuba's beaches.

Kennedy had been ill-advised by the generals once before. They assured him, early in his administration, that a CIA-orchestrated invasion to overthrow Castro at Cuba's Bay of Pigs would work. He gave the go-ahead. Castro savaged the invading CIA-sponsored Cuban exiles at Bahia de Cochinos (Bay of Pigs), killing and capturing most of them and humiliating the young president. Admitting his blunder in trusting his military commanders, Mr. Kennedy apologized for the mistake, saying, "Success has a hundred fathers, defeat is an orphan." Kennedy did not have much faith in his commanders ever again.

He and Khrushchev made a secret deal for U.S. removal of its missiles in Turkey in exchange for the Soviet missile pullout in Cuba. Diplomacy, not military action, prevailed. It was the ultimate close call that alerted atomic powers not to use nuclear brinksmanship as a tool to get their way.

President Bill Clinton faced another, much smaller, crisis over Cuba. Fidel was livid because airplanes out of south Florida were flying over Havana and dropping anti-Castro leaflets. Castro shook a finger at Washington, demanding repeatedly that Clinton stop the pirate over-flights. Castro knew the small, twin-engine Cessnas flying illegally over his country were piloted by his archenemies in exile. A former CIA operative, José Basulto, was the chief of *Hermanos de Rescate* (Brothers to the Rescue), a Miami-based activist organization dedicated to the overthrow of the Cuban dictator. Trained in explosives, sabotage and subversion by the CIA, Basulto was long known for his rabid opposition to Communist Cuba, where he was born.

I'd been following the dangerous Cuba vs. America drama for years, having traveled to Havana more than 100 times by February 24, 1996. On that day, a Cuban-piloted MiG 29 blew two of the unarmed Cessnas out of the sky with air-to-air missiles. Four Americans were killed, but Basulto got

187

away, flying his Cessna into a cloud cover to avoid the Cuban combat jet. Still, the pilot of the heavily armed MiG radioed his glee over the downing, congratulating himself and his *"cojones."* Madeline Albright, U.S. Ambassador to the U.N., condemned the brutal air attack and the MiG pilot. "Frankly this is not *cojones,"* she said. "This is cowardice."

Just days before the bring-down, Cuba's diplomat, José Ponce, bemoaned to me the unlawful intrusions into Cuban air space by the exile aircraft. We were sitting alone in an anteroom at the Cuban Interests Section, the old Cuban Embassy, in Washington, D.C.
"We don't know what to do," Ponce fretted. "We have asked your president to stop. But he ignores us. What would you do?"

Startled by his question, I absentmindedly responded: "Well, why don't you just shoot them down?" I think Ponce took me seriously. But I didn't give my off-hand comment any thought until my beeper went off in Key West, Florida, where I was on vacation. Key West is only 90 miles from Havana, and I was closer to the attack than most reporters.

The shattering news alarmed me, instantly, that the careless remark I'd made to Ponce had become the stuff of an international incident. If my unseemly statement was taken into consideration by the Cuban government in deliberations on how to respond to their enemy's air incursion, I may never know. I do know, now, that Cuba's top leadership followed avidly my coverage of their government for tell-tale signs emanating from America's military and intelligence community. As a reporter, I did have CIA connections and, at the time of the MiG attack, I was the Pentagon correspondent for NBC.

My contacts in Cuba, cultivated over years of reporting from there, served me well when I went back to Havana, once more, to cover the aftermath of the air-to-air clash. Fidel and I were on a first-name basis. Cuba's deputy foreign minister, Carlos Fernandez de Cossio, enlisted my help to establish a hotline between the Pentagon and Cuba to help avert another military confrontation. As a response to the MiG attack, President Clinton considered launching cruise missiles to destroy Cuba's airbase at San Antonio de los Baños near Havana. The MiG that killed the Americans was based there.

Cuba is ready for us if we ever attack. Throughout the island, deep underground tunnels contain long lines of tanks and artillery pieces poised to throw the Americans back into the sea. Explosive mines sit at idle waiting to be cast upon the Straits of Florida to blow our ships to smithereens should it ever come to that.

At a hidden camp in Pinar del Rio, militarily fit special forces teams practice tactics to emerge from their live burial places in beach sand to take out our troops coming ashore.

Despite their toughness, the Cubans are no match for the U.S., according to General John Sheehan, who is the former Supreme Allied Commander and Commander-in-Chief, U.S. Atlantic Command. Cuban-Americans in Miami denounced General Sheehan because he belittled Castro's ability to mount attacks against Cuba's neighbors. The Miamians were furious with General Sheehan for telling me, on-camera, that Cuba was no threat to the United States or anybody else.

Castro was all huff and puff according to the Pentagon. Still, Castro can puff himself up in front of the cameras or even when his back is turned. Then Chairman of the Joint Chiefs, General John Shalikashvili , welcomed the idea of a hotline. But he told me the White House would never go for it. Shalikashvili thought the U.S. should normalize relations with Cuba. So did most of the generals.

Such an unprecedented contact with Communist Cuba, a hotline, was out of the question for political reasons. To this day the U.S. lists Cuba as a state sponsor of terrorism. Castro is in the company of Iran, Sudan and Syria, not for acts of terrorism. Cuba is on the list in order to placate anti-Castro die-hards in Miami.

Almost every Cuban-American I've met is immersed in the belief he left a fortune behind when he or his forebears fled Fidel. Descriptions of the fincas, the estates abandoned in their flight for freedom are beyond belief. There aren't enough farm houses left in all of Cuba to validate the claims of a tenth of those who want their money back. Most of the Cubans who came here are ordinary people who've been given extraordinary benefits, paid for by the rest of us. Our government established special categories to give Cubans a foot up over other immigrants who have to wait in line. If a Cuban rafter can put his foot on dry land here, we let him in automatically. Tough luck if you are a Haitian or any other poor slob trying to escape the hell holes of the Caribbean. I'll tell you this: the blessings of liberty are wasted on all those Cuban-Americans who thumb their noses at our Constitution and our democratic institutions. Of course, they wouldn't know anything about that, having supported despots back home.

The fevered anti-communism of the '60s set up the special status for Cubans on the lam. But tilting at windmills is out of fashion in the 21st century. Castro is a toothless tiger waiting to die. His old Soviet sponsors are dead already. U.S. policy toward Cuba is antiquated, way out of date. It is that policy that denies you the right to spend time and money in Cuba if you want. Isn't that silly?

Cuban-Americans hold the rest of us captive to get a kidnapper's ransom. Theirs is the rip-off of the century. They almost snatched Elián González from his father, until President Clinton stepped in. In 2000, some fishermen in the Straits of Florida had found Elián González, that sweet little Cuban kid who had been set adrift on an inner tube. His mom had died by drowning on their fateful sea voyage from Cuba to America. Elián survived, miraculously.

No sooner had Elián been discharged from a Miami hospital in amazingly good health, when in swooped Cuban-American Congressmen to use the poor little tyke to their advantage. They wrapped Elián in the American flag, literally, and dared Clinton to send him home to his dad. When Mr. Clinton's attorney general, Janet Reno, said we would follow the law of the land and give the child back, Miami erupted in protest. The law be damned! Blood was in their eyes as they shut down their city, burned the American flag and generally acted like the thugs they are. Flag burning by right wing extremists in Miami must give pause to those who want a Constitutional amendment banning the immolation of the stars and stripes. The irony is palpable. I never heard any right wingers—those who would be identified as Tea Partiers today—protesting against their Cuban brothers for sending the flag up in flames. Flag desecration, I guess, is okay when the ringleaders are on your team. And defying the law is absolutely intolerable, unless, of course, your conservative cause is just. Then burn, baby, burn! The hypocrisy of the right in America is not just scary; it's possibly criminal. The founding fathers were correct in erecting Constitutional barriers to frustrate those who would take our guns away while, simultaneously, granting all citizens the right to set the American flag on fire. The "right to bear arms" and the right of "freedom of speech"—flag desecration—are contemporaneous Constitutional guarantees. Be thankful you have them.

The shelf life of the Castro rebellion ran out long ago, the expiration date stamped when Fidel triumphed on January 1, 1959, the same year Buddy Holly's music died. That year Holly released his last record, and American Airlines inaugurated the first transcontinental jet, LA to NY ($301).

Cuba never has been free. It just exchanged one dictator for another in '59. Washington's SOB, Fulgencio Batista, was out; the Kremlin's SOB, Fidel Castro, was in. When you hear Havana Radio on short wave announce, *Estaes Radio Havana, Cuba, transmitiendodes de Cuba, territorio libre en Las Americas,* take it for what it's worth. A real sovereign doesn't require justification from one super power or the other. Autonomy, by definition, stands alone on its own two feet. Without Soviet support, Cuba was and always would be just another American lackey. The Soviets bought Cuba as a military base and spy station for about $5,000,000,000—that's $5-billion with a B—annually, until President Mikhail Gorbachev showed up in Havana on April 3, 1989, to cut the purse strings. In a come-to-Jesus meeting, Gorbachev withdrew his economic support, leaving Castro to fend for himself. He advised Castro to "integrate the island into the Western Hemisphere's economy." What is more, Cuba was no longer under the Soviet nuclear umbrella. The door was wide open for a U.S. military attack, tacitly canceling a promise made by President Kennedy to the Soviets that the U.S. would never invade Cuba.

In the back of his mind, I assume, Castro knew he was not his own man, that he was a kept woman. He rejected the idea of being a puppet, but every time Moscow told him to jump, Castro would ask, "How high?" The ultimate humiliation for Castro came on the day during the 1963 missile crisis when Khrushchev gave in to Kennedy with not so much as a nod toward Fidel. Castro's counterfeit position was exposed to the entire world.

When I interviewed him shortly after Gorbachev left town and left Castro holding the bag, he admitted Cuba would have to change its socialist ways. He would inaugurate a "special period," Castro said, to overcome the economic disaster his country faced. During the "special period," Cuba almost foundered.

Castro may be revered by his countrymen, but he knows he is reviled by his enemies. One day I walked with him to his luxury Mercedes-Benz S-500 sedan. As an aide opened the rear door to let Castro enter, I noticed in a web pocket, within Castro's reach, what appeared to be an Uzi machine gun. Castro always carried a holstered pistol on his web belt. And he wore a bullet-proof vest. *Comandante-en-Jefe* (Commander-in-Chief) was dressed, as usual, in his olive green fatigues and signature green military cap.

But his beard was becoming gray and scraggly. So was his revolution. In his later years, Castro became a cliché. Not only was his revolution suffering from a mid-life crisis, it had entered the twilight zone of worthlessness. Once a model for Latin American revolutionaries, Castro's insurgency had become irrelevant. Right wing military dictators turned to democracy for legitimacy. Revolutionaries were no longer a threat. About the only friend Castro could count on was the leftist Hugo Chavez of Venezuela. But even Chavez was democratically elected. There had been no free and fair election for the Cuban presidency since Castro took over in January 1959. He will be a dictator, hating America, until the day he dies.

In one of our last interviews, I asked Castro why he did not step down to allow younger Cubans to take over. The fragile Fidel answered me with his pat speech about being a warrior fighting still in defense of the fatherland. The old man, at age 85, had begun to limp, his gait unsure.

Although honored at home, he was a grandfather figure beloved by his countrymen, not for soldiering on, but for having thumbed his nose at the United States time after time.

He paid lip service to a policy to groom younger men and women for the presidency. Yet he never trusted anyone not in his inner circle to keep pure his antiquated revolt. In one of his last appointments, Castro promoted José Ramon Machado, an 80-year-old crony *historico* to the second highest post in the powerful Cuban Communist Party. The *historicos* are the old men and women who fought for and alongside Castro in his 1950s revolution in the Sierra Maestra.

Castro's brother, Raul, also an octogenarian, inherited the title of president. But until Fidel Castro dies, there probably will not be a complete power transfer. That probability begs the question: What happens after Fidel dies?

Don't look for a liberal democracy to arise. Don't pack your bags for a trip to Cuba any time soon. Keep your notion of retirement in a balmy dreamland "*De donde crecen la Palma*"—keep that fantasy on hold. The elderly who will remain in power are likely to perpetuate a slightly modified Castroism. They will continue to blame the United States for all their problems, which are massive—poverty, economic stagnation, lack of opportunity, gross mismanagement, human rights violations to name just a few.

None of these are Cuba's pleasure, they will argue. America's long-established hostile policy toward Havana is to blame, the elders will say. If it weren't for the decades-old economic embargo against Cuba, they will declare, their island would flourish. Hardly. But it is a good argument that has helped keep the Castros and their cronies in power for so long.

If it weren't for the distress caused by the embargo, the contention goes, the terror and horror suffered by those who try to escape on rafts would not occur. Washington claims Cubans flee their homeland for political reasons. They are so desperate to get out of the swamp of Communism, Washington's line of reasoning goes, they risk their lives on the high seas to get to America. Havana claims the flood of immigrants outbound would end as soon as the embargo is lifted. This is such an unpleasant fiction.

The truth is Cubans on both sides of the Straits of Florida are engaged in a Kabuki dance. Cuban exiles in Florida and Cuban Communists in Havana have been locked in a symbiotic relationship for a very long time. Entire livelihoods based on Fidel-bashing thrive in Miami, where virulent anti-Castro radio transmissions bore to tears anybody who is not among the rabidly faithful. If one does not agree with the exile party line, he is liable to be bashed himself.

In Havana, the party could not be happier. As long as the Marxist despots have a reason to verbally attack the U.S., they will fare well. The party instills fear in the populace by warning that the Cuban-Americans want to return and take their homes and their dignity away from them. The exiles and Washington are the bogeyman, always ready to pounce. Washington could put an end to the foolishness in a nano-second by simply restoring normal relations with Havana. After all, we have normal diplomatic and trade relations with Communist China. We have normal diplomatic and trade relations with Communist Vietnam, where 55 thousand Americans died in the Vietnam War.

As much sense as it makes to normalize, Washington is not about to do it. Any administration, Democrat or Republican, that tried would be instantly branded as "unfriendly" by South Florida's huge exile community, one million strong. "So what?" you ask. Well the "so what" is contained in their ability to deny to either party the U.S. Presidency. Florida has 27 electoral votes. Without those votes, presidential aspirants can kiss their aspirations goodbye. Cuban-Americans take pride in being able to manipulate the vote for president any way they want to. Just ask Al Gore. So what if the rest of us are held hostage by their petulance?

It is high time for the Cuban-Americans to get over it. The way to get back to Cuba is to make nice. That'll be the day.

V
Lies and Deceptions

31
Hatred for Truth Tellers

Sadness is a wall between two gardens.
—Kahlil Gibran

Everywhere I have gone, I have seen it in their eyes.
Hate—pure unadulterated malevolence. Arabs hate us. We
hate the Arabs. Israelis hate the Arabs. The Arabs hate the
Israelis. The Chinese hate the Japanese. The Japanese
hate the Vietnamese. The Vietnamese hate the Chinese.
And the Chinese hate them right back. Well, you get the
picture.

I stopped off in Japan on my way to Vietnam in 1970. Two
stories awaited me in my hop off. My mission was to
expose the Japanese for their indefensible whale hunts and
to out their mismanagement at Minamata. The Japanese
hated me for it. That's what happens when you tell the
truth. People hate you for it. Let me count the ways. Well, I
can't because it would take too long.

Minamata is a small town about 570 miles southwest of
Tokyo. Farmers and fishermen and their families live there
on Minamata Bay. When Chisso Corporation dumped
massive amounts of mercury into the bay, thousands of
inhabitants of Minamata unexpectedly developed
symptoms of methyl mercury poisoning. The mercury was
waste from Chisso's operation. The people gave the
dumping little thought, at first.
First, the town cats were hit after eating the fish drying in
the sun. Fish from the bay constituted the main diet of the
townspeople and their cats. People thought their cats were
going insane because the felines committed suicide. Later,

198

birds began falling from the sky. The unexplained sickness in the cats and the birds brought panic to Minamata. People began to notice the "strange disease" had hit them, too. Numbness occurred in their limbs and lips. Their speech became slurred, and their vision constricted. Some shouted uncontrollably. Others lapsed into unconsciousness. Doctors saw serious brain damage and finally made their diagnosis. Minamata disease was a killer that left those who survived with gross physical deformities. Children were born without extremities. Horrified mothers untouched by the disease gave birth to babies disfigured and stunted.

Ultimately the people took Chisso to court when the company denied responsibility. By that time, more than 3,000 victims were dead or dying. Chisso finally owned up to its utter disregard for the health of Minamata and its own workers who lived in town. But the company and its lawyers were still back peddling when I arrived in 1970. Chisso was holding out on granting payments to the victims when we turned on the spotlight. Though the news went viral and the world was shocked, the Japanese were obstinate still. Alerted by the dreadful pictures of victims in Minamata, communities in the United States and around the world took precautions and warned against mercury poisoning. That was progress, but as late as 1993—23 years after our story aired—the Japanese courts were still resolving suitable compensation for the victims. Meanwhile, many people continue suffering to this day from the physical and emotional pain of Minamata Disease.

Japanese, like Americans, don't enjoy being reminded about their blunders. In fact, they hate those who are the reminders. But we keep on, relentlessly.

…for there is no folly of the beast of the earth which is not infinitely outdone by the madness of men.

—Herman Melville, *Moby Dick*

I was astonished when the Japanese let us board one of their whaling ships with our cameras. Maybe they were naïve. Or perhaps they wanted to explain to the global community why they continued to hunt whales to extinction. Whatever the case, it did not work for them.

As Walter Cronkite wrote in his impressive *Eye on The World,* "Of all the creatures on this earth, none is more generally revered, feared, and wondered at than the whale. He is, along with man, woman and firmament, [located] in the Book of Genesis: 'And God created great whales.'" He continued:

> This far along the road toward whatever ultimate end, the whale—his symbolic servitude not yet over—offers himself as an embodiment, a vast and archetypal monarch as symbol of the deeps that were all our beginnings, being edged toward extinction by a creature more cunning if less wise.

> The story of the whale in our time is almost too perfect an analogy: He is mighty, ageless, and in great trouble. Man, a conqueror seemingly unaware how close he himself is to the same fate, wages his war through a technology he cannot control. We can save the whale or kill him; save ourselves or commit suicide.

> We know the alternatives; we have the means.

For those of you who missed it, here is the text of my report recounting the three days I spent aboard a Japanese whaling ship as broadcast on *The CBS Evening News* with Cronkite:

200

Ed Rabel: We are sailing out of the Japanese port of Ayukawa into the North Pacific aboard a whaling ship equipped with a cannon high upon the bow. Within the barrel there is a whaling harpoon with a bomb in its head. Soon it will be fired into the body of the largest of all sea creatures, and there it will explode, and the leviathan will die. Standing there beside the powerful gun, the wind at your face, there are recollections of a time when men died while stalking whales, of small harpoons piercing the sides of giant, spouting mammals. But aboard the diesel whale catcher *Tashimaru,* capable of seventeen knots and equipped with electronic eyes and ears and a cannon mounted at its peak, even the great white sperm whale, the hero monster of Moby Dick, with the largest brain of any animal, would be no match.

Soon we are upon the whales, a dozen or more swimming and spouting. Koki Huntuwa, who has stood for fourteen years at the trigger lever of a harpoon gun, has taken command. While directing the movements of the highly maneuverable boat using a small microphone mounted in the gun, Huntuwa's squinting eyes are fixed on the now frightened animals.

Huntuwa has killed his first whale of the day. But he has made a mistake; the mortally wounded animal is a female with her calf alongside. Whaling rules prohibit killing females with calves. As the whale is pulled nearby, the calf swims protectively around her. Then, almost as if sensing the hopelessness of the situation, the calf swims away. A huge rubber float, a radio buoy, and a radar reflector with the whaling company's identifying flag are shackled to the corpse. The dead whale is then set adrift, to be picked up when the day's hunt is done.

The gunner commands the ship to return to the hunt, for the whales have taken flight. Whales, like humans, must breathe, and these frightened whales, like frightened humans, gasp for breath. But they cannot outrun the fast boat, and the killing resumes. At the end of the hunt the *Tashimaru* returns to pick up the catch. One of the whales, thought to be dead, has survived and is swimming away with the attached radar reflector pinpointing its location. The boat must pursue. The whale is overtaken and harpooned once again. It is learned the whale has swum six miles from where it was originally harpooned. Working quickly, the crew picks up each whale, lashing them to the side of the boat. The floats and flags are also retrieved and stowed for another hunt to come the next day.

For the crew of *The Tashimaru*, the hunt has been a big success. Two-and-a-half hours after the whales were spotted, ten of them had been harpooned, and in less than a day from our departure we are headed back to port, the whales at our side.

Fears that whales are being hunted to extinction are reinforced by observing the efficiency of this whaling ship. In the past decade alone, 607,000 whales have been slaughtered, mostly by the Japanese and Russians. Altogether, the three major whaling companies killed 61 sperm whales on this day. The number slaughtered by the Tayo Company's three boats was 29 sperm whales. It is estimated the day's catch is worth $11,000. Whales are processed into margarine, soap, hand cream, suntan oil, lipstick, paint dryer, cat and dog food, shoe polish, and fertilizer. But of all the products of whales, meat is the most important to the Japanese. They will eat 127,000 tons of whale meat this year. It would seem the laws of economics would eventually force the Japanese to stop whaling, but, although the international demand for whale products is dropping and substitutes for most whale products are readily available, Japan's whalers insist they must go on killing whales, just to satisfy their country's demand for the meat.

Today a whale is killed every twelve minutes. So intensive is the slaughter that some scientists say no sperm whale ever dies of old age. The argument is frequently heard that our environmental crisis will solve itself because, as industry faces the end of its raw materials, it will become more careful, will conserve and protect the resources it now destroys. The recent history of the whaling industry offers little hope for that theory.

The Japanese hated us for telling that story, too. They threatened me and my producer, Red Cross, by sending government officials to confront us in the Tokyo bureau. A lot of bowing and scraping transpired as the officials demanded an apology. We did not say I'm sorry. And the story aired time and time again. It is on the air today, an emblem of the worldwide movement for a better environment.

32
Mutual Memories

Yesterday, December 7, 1941—a date which will live on in infamy …
—U.S. President Franklin Delano Roosevelt

We have been at odds with the Japanese for a long time. December 7, of course, "is a date which will live in infamy." President Franklin Delano Roosevelt said so following the Japanese sneak attack on Pearl Harbor that killed or wounded 3,581 Americans. Four years later, President Harry Truman dropped the atomic bomb on Hiroshima and Nagasaki, on the Japanese mainland. We killed hundreds of thousands of Japanese citizens in those attacks. It is argued we saved a million lives by bringing the war with the Japanese to an abrupt end. Otherwise, entire divisions of American and Japanese troops might have been wiped out in a bloody slug-fest on a string of islands in the South Pacific in the allied move to capture the Japanese mainland. The Japanese will never forget what happened. Neither will America.

On December 7, 1980, the Japanese remembered still. So did we. It's *Sunday Morning* on CBS, and here again are Charles Kuralt and Ed Rabel, in a transcript abbreviated for the reader. Newsreels from the period and Japanese commercials for products are part of the story.

> Kuralt: The Japanese didn't want to trade with the United States in the first place. Commodore Perry steamed into Tokyo Bay in 1853 and trained the guns of his naval squadron on the emperor's

palace to force them to trade. Perry gave the emperor of Japan a telescope, a miniature locomotive, a hundred-and-ten gallons of whiskey, eight baskets of potatoes, and four volumes of Audubon's *Birds of America.* The emperor gave Perry 500 bushels of rice, 300 chickens, 20 umbrellas and 13 dolls. And if you want to know where that flood of Sonys and Hondas started, that's where. It is Sunday, December 7, and time for a little more Japanese-American history, as Ed Rabel reports our *Sunday Morning* cover story.

Rabel: It is dawn at Pearl Harbor on Sunday morning, 39 years ago today. Japanese pilots, in their Nakajima and Aichi bombers and Kaga and Mitsubishi fighters, are systematically killing Americans. Killed or wounded are 3,581 Americans, half of them U.S. Bluejackets on the battleship *Arizona.* For the time being, the United States Navy is virtually eliminated by the treacherous, single, sharp blow.

President Franklin Delano Roosevelt: Yesterday, December 7, 1941, a date which will live in infamy, the United States of America was suddenly and deliberately attacked. I ask that the Congress declare a state of war has existed between the United States and the Japanese Empire.

Newsreel Reporter: The mad Japanese dog strikes in the Pacific, and Washington's State Department gives the incredible news to reporters who had been awaiting news of peace negotiations with the sly, war-crazed Japs. ... Emperor Hirohito leads the LYBs, the little yellow-bellies, who claim the rising sun for their own.

Rabel: The attack on Pearl Harbor is a psychological blunder for Japan, because it unites the Americans, who are fed a diet of racist propaganda. ...President Roosevelt signs an executive order condemning 110,000 Japanese-Americans to barbed-wire detention camps simply because they look like the enemy: different, distrusted, feared. No such order is issued for German-Americans or Italian-Americans.

Former detainee Tom Hoshiyama: We knew it was wrong to put us in camp, and yet we did not open our mouth to even say how I ... we felt, in fear of many things. ... I couldn't get a haircut in a barber shop. I couldn't go to the skating rink. I couldn't go to the swimming pool. That's the kind of atmosphere I was brought up in when I first moved here. Today it's entirely different. There isn't a place that I can't get into, regardless of my looks.

Rabel: ... America is not proud of the way it treated these people. Americans are revolted by the racism, puzzled by the virulence. After all, two-thirds of Americans were born after Pearl Harbor Day, and they don't remember. Over the years, they have grown to love and admire things Japanese. *Shogun*, the story of a Japan ruled by war lords, was a big hit on U.S. television. Americans eat Japanese food. They learn how to defend themselves Japanese-style. But most of all, Americans have a high regard for quality cars and cameras and stereos and electronic gadgets and TV sets. Most American households have at least two or three expensive Japanese products. But now that Japanese goods are flooding the U.S. Market, a love-hate relationship seems to be developing between some Americans and some Japanese. ...The American automotive industry blames much of its woes on Japanese imported cars and trucks. The chairman of the Ford Motor Company, Philip Caldwell, tried but failed to persuade the U.S. International Trade Commission to set quotas and higher import duties on the Japanese.

Automaker Philip Caldwell: This country cannot afford the continuing exploitation of our automotive market by the Japanese, which will now be worsened by the effective steps being

208

taken by European and other countries to limit the importation of Japanese cars and trucks into their markets.

Rabel: Latent resentment is being triggered by Japan's assertiveness, especially where steel mills are shut down and auto plants are idle. We don't call them Japs or Nips or little yellow-bellies or sly or war-crazed anymore, but the renewal of anti-Japanese feeling is real. The Japanese, calling it racially inspired, are fighting back.

Nippon Steel vice president Kiichi Mochizuki [who was a child when planes struck Pearl Harbor]: Americans cannot be the best in every area. You have to allow other people to be pretty good in some areas, and you are pretty good in other areas. … I understand that Americans have been very accustomed to the … what people call Pax Americana. Since 1945, American industry, as well as other things, has been very, very predominant in the world. And they have become so accustomed to it, in a sense spoiled by that, that it is hard … so hard for Americans to accept that somebody else may be better in some areas. I would like you to prepare your states of mind to accept that healthy and… and … and live in this world together with other people. So just closing up your country and just attack other people … peoples and … and be too tight about it and so forth ... I don't think it's healthy. It's not good for your health.

Rabel: So, the consumer products keep coming. Datsuns and Toyotas cover the docks in Japan, standing ready for delivery to a receptive American market. Japan has not transformed itself from a defeated island community into the second most productive nation in the world by hanging back.

Mochizuki: The industrial ability, capacity, is not the physical plant; it's people—the managerial, technological ability of the nation. And you didn't kill ... kill all Japanese; that's why we're here.

Rabel: Pearl Harbor is still an unbearable memory for the American families who lost their men in Hawaii and in the savage island battles of the Pacific war. Many of them will never forget or forgive. ... Edwin Reischauer, whose brother was killed in Shanghai during the war, was ambassador to Japan in the sixties.

Reishauer: You have some people ... strictly among older people ... who have memories of World War II, and our feelings are very, very bitter indeed. ... And you have a greater tendency, an easier sense of suspicion or distaste for people who are physically quite different from us, the majority of the United ... people in the United States.

And this shows up much more easily than it would with Europeans, who are so much more like us. This is the … the thing that underlies the whole problem of race. But again, as compared with a few decades ago, we've so tremendously changed on these points that I just cannot see a reversal of this tendency towards a gradual blurring of this feeling of race in this country.

Rabel to Mochizuki: Do you think the Japanese and the Americans, then, will ever be able to really understand one another? We are rather alien to one another, of course.

Mochizuki: Yes, well, let's take 200 years to solve this problem.

Rabel: That long?

Mochizuki: Well, I … I thought it was rather short.

Rabel: You think it would take 200 years to solve the problem?

Mochizuki: Solve the racial problems all over the world, and 200 years is a very optimistic, short time.

Rabel: In the meantime, Japanese and Americans alike come here to this memorial at Pearl Harbor to remember and reflect. And the question invariably arises: Could our differences prompt us to do awful things to one another as we did before, here and at Hiroshima and Nagasaki? Not likely, the experts say, for both sides have come too far and have too much at stake to ever let anything like that happen again. Japanese economic aggressiveness and arrogance, they explain, is something we can—we must—live with.

Reischauer: They're arrogant in many ways because they're doing so well. But this is an arrogance that is beginning to balance the tremendous arrogance of the white race towards the non-white race. Maybe it's a good thing for us to have the Japanese a little arrogant for a while. And this will sort of help balance things up on both sides. They've got a lot to overcome themselves. You know, an inferiority complex, because for over a hundred years they've been just trying to catch desperately up with us. And this has left some very deep scars on them that have to be worn away. Well, feeling arrogant, on top of things, will probably help in that way, and I think it'll help us to be a little bit more modest and learn maybe to handle our relations with other non-Western people better.

Today, more than three decades since my stories on Japan aired, the American-Japanese relationship has grown stronger. American technology in automobiles and computers rival the Japanese, who are no longer dominant in electronics. Japan, like America, has suffered as a global economic powerhouse. It remains an ever-increasingly important ally in the Asian rim, where Communist China has become the prime global dynamo on which the U.S. is focused. As the U.S. builds up its military forces in the region to check China's growing influence, Japan is likely to be the first line of defense and offense if China acts on its aggressive rhetoric.

33
Giddy Up Horse—A Mountaineer in The Holy Land

No culture can live, if it attempts to be exclusive.
—Mahatma Gandhi

Israel has one foot in history, its hands full of today and its fingers crossed for tomorrow. Entering the Promised Land is like staring at the sun, for you are blinded by the dazzling reminiscences of antiquity overlaid with incomparable modernity. While turning outward, with its arms open to the Diaspora, Israel faces away from its foes, containing itself in its own mystery. A cacophonous atmosphere of temperance and intemperance accosted me when I arrived in Tel Aviv in 1971 for a three-year tour of duty. Childhood dreams or nightmares about the birthplace and crucifixion of the Savior became a stunning veracity. The Bible was no longer a theory.

Arab awe in the Dome of The Rock and Jewish dread at the Wailing Wall depicted the centralization of world religion in Jerusalem. There were constant reminders of the focus of humanity. Deep within humankind's DNA is the beginning from the same Father.

There rose up within me, then, a perplexity that questioned how so many of us could have died killing so many of us within the religious context. When I witnessed the bloody Twin Towers and compared it with what happened in places like Hiroshima, I saw the horrifying truth that none of us is ever going to get out of this alive.

And I invited derision born of complacency when I postulated the theory there could be a happy ending. Naysayers scoffed when I reminded them we all inhabit the same planet. We all breathe the same air. We all cherish our children and their futures. Universal forgiveness is in all of us if we can only accept it. In the eternal struggle we are annihilating ourselves. Look carefully and you will see we have the same face, the same blood, and the same feet to walk on common ground. Rich, poor, short, tall, red, yellow, black or white. They are us and we reject them. They are the faces of our own damned future.

As a rock-ribbed Baptist in the midst of such holy mixture, I was left wondering about why the things uniting us do not outweigh the things dividing us. T.S. Eliot got me just right: "Oh my soul…be prepared for him who knows how to ask questions." I was never prepared for myself. Too many things are left unanswered.

On May 8, 1972, terrorists hijacked a Sabena Airlines Boeing 707 loaded with passengers and landed it in the heart of Israel at Tel Aviv International, right in front of our cameras. Were they out of their minds? Another one of those persistent questions. Their demands were straightforward. All they wanted was to replace the passengers on board with about 80 of their brothers held in Israeli jails. That's all they wanted.

In broad daylight, in front of my camera, the Israeli Defense Forces disabled the jet by flattening its tires in a hail of bullets. For three days, out of sight at the airport, IDF Special Forces, including the current Prime Minister Benjamin Netanyahu, practiced a rescue operation. Israel was ready for the seven fanatics in the plane. Netanyahu was serving with distinction as an officer in the Israeli Defense Forces when the hijacking occurred. He rose to

215

the rank of captain in the IDF following the 1973 Yom Kippur War.

"Benny," as his friends call him, organized two international conferences against terrorism (1979 and 1984) that attracted participation from world leaders, including former U.S. President George Bush and former U.S. Secretary of State George Shultz.

The hijacking ended in a burst of gunfire and killing. The hijackers aboard the plane watched anxiously, unaware they would die within moments. They fell for the inspired trap about to be sprung. Defense force personnel disguised as Red Cross workers approached the aircraft. In their white out-coats emblazoned with the Red Cross and hiding their lethality, the sly soldiers placed ladders against the Sabena fuselage so they could launch their assault.

Within thirty seconds the Israelis boarded the plane, set off flash grenades and gunned down all seven of the heavily armed skyjackers. Nearly all of the passengers were saved. The spectacular operation was carried off right in front of our cameras. That's how confident the Israelis were that they would succeed. Moreover, the Israelis sent a message to others who would threaten them. Don't do it. If anti-Israeli militants arrayed throughout the world saw the tarmac demonstration, they either didn't get the message or ignored it completely.

Not long afterward, on May 30, 1972, my cameramen and I were back at Lod Airport (now Ben Gurion International) to witness the aftermath of yet another attack. Three members of the Japanese Red Army Faction, an offshoot of the bloody German Beider-Meinhof Gang, had killed 26 and wounded 80 others. The three Japanese men—on behalf of the PFLP, the Popular Front for the Liberation of Palestine—had arrived on Air France flight 132. Once inside the airport's baggage claim area, the three, dressed conservatively, opened violin cases they hand-carried. Out came Czech vz.58 assault rifles they used to spray the crowded zone. It did not end well for the three terrorists. One of them was shot dead by Israeli guards, the second purposely exploded a grenade he'd put under his chin, and the third was wounded by the Israelis. He was sentenced to life in an Israeli prison.

Israel was ready, again, four years later at Entebbe airport in Uganda. Throughout history Israel has paid the price for its exclusivity. That's why there is perpetual trouble in paradise.

On July 4, 1976, Israeli commandoes flew all the way to Entebbe from Israel in C-130s loaded with the uncanny liberators and special automobiles. A black Mercedes-Benz with accompanying Land Rovers were taken along to outwit the terrorists, who held a hundred Jews and Israelis hostage. Non-Jews had been released by the hijackers of the Air France flight. The IDF used an Idi Amin look-alike in the fantastic rescue operation. Idi Amin was the murderous Ugandan tyrant who helped the fanatics. They thought the convoy was official, bearing Amin in his Mercedes to the airport to congratulate them. Were *they* surprised. The commandos pounced on them and liberated the hostages in a barrage of gunfire. The hostages were safe, but Benjamin Netanyahu's brother, Yoni, an IDF officer, was killed during the action.

In early1978, Wadie Haddad, the primary organizer of the May 8, 1972, attack, was assassinated by Mossad, Israel's super effective CIA. America would learn much from Mossad's methods—but not enough to prevent the 2001 multiple skyjackings that ended in the massacre of more than 3,000 people in New York, Washington and Pennsylvania. Failure of imagination permitted terrorists to

217

hijack airplanes they deliberately flew into the Twin Towers in New York, the Pentagon outside Washington, D.C., and a field in Pennsylvania. We simply could not or would not envision such unmitigated horror.

Imagination is something the Israelis have in abundance. Yet in spite of their historical imperative—or perhaps because of it—Israel is bound by the Bible to obliteration. There is always trouble in paradise. But all is not lost. Incongruity, embedded in another Israel, surprises visitors expecting nothing but holy history that inspires bloody conflict.

Looking for another fight for CBS News, your reporter encountered a different kind of gunplay, Israel's version of *Shootout at the OK Corral*. Horse operas are a mainstay of Israel's flourishing film industry. Israel's multifaceted landscape, from vast deserts to lush highlands of flowers and grasses to snow-covered mountains, perfect in their majesty, lends itself flawlessly to film makers. Out on the plains, horsemen followed by cameras and bright lights and makeup artists can be seen riding into the sunset. But instead of spurring their steeds with the traditional "giddy up," cowboys here shout out instead, "Shalom horse!"

Anti-Semite! Wretched goy! Ignorant hillbilly! Those are the printable expletives I had to endure for using "Shalom horse" as a tag line in a TV piece on Israel's unexpected foray into filmdom—a minor controversy over what my fans and I reasoned to be hilarious. Lighten up.

Then there was Christmas in Bethlehem, on the outskirts of Jerusalem. Here I was, walking holy ground and nearly paralyzed by its significance. In the time of Christ, Bethlehem was BeitLehem, David's City, and the location of his crowning as the King of Israel. Jerusalem, where Christ was crucified, was known as Yerushalayim ("Abode

218

of Peace") in Hebrew and Al-Quds ("The Holy Sanctuary") in Arabic.

If you are in Jericho, at the Dead Sea, Palestinian taxi drivers can be heard to this day pandering for passengers by shouting out, "Al-Quds! Al-Quds, Al-Quds, Al-Quds! Just 30 minutes away!"

Today pilgrims stream into Bethlehem to sing praises to the marvelous Christian holiday marking the birth of Christ. In the Church of the Nativity, I was assailed by my personal images of how it must have been on that starry, starry night when God's messenger of total love appeared on the scene. No way, I thought, could I convey adequately on television the majesty and simplicity of the blessed site that stirs the soul of man. My duty here was not the unmasking of villains. A reaffirmation of man's potential for mercy, a retelling of that ancient story of hope for mankind was my responsibility. *Do not fall short*, I told myself.

Yet I could not ignore the distortions I saw. Israel's gunmen patrolling rooftops spoiled the sacred setting. They were there, of course, to safeguard antique artifacts and present-day pilgrims. This was, in spite of everything, occupied land. The ubiquitous presence of snipers prompted my cynicism to arise in my reports. This is a place that may never see peace.

The very old town was not without its mild charm, too. A mostly Palestinian town, then, it catered to outsiders who thirsted for all reminders of their own fundamental beliefs. A hand-crafted Nativity scene made in Bethlehem was much in demand and highly prized. Back home, the pilgrims could point with pride to their treasured work of art advertised by Bethlehem's shop owners as carefully crafted, handmade masterpieces. But in the back rooms of those shops we found and filmed the Nativity scenes being

219

carved by the truckloads on mass production machines. Visit Bethlehem today and linger in awe in "Manger Square" if you want to see kitsch defined.

An exposé is an exposé, in all things great and small. The little sin in Bethlehem was passed by satellite to New York and went on the air at CBS alongside all the other news of the day. Mine was the first-ever report to be transmitted by satellite from Al-Quds. Whether the pettiness of the incident merited the attention it was given is not the point. If someone runs a stop light or commits murder, there must be an accounting.

In his fictionalized account of the JFK assassination, *11/22/63*, Stephen King wrote: "There are no single crimes. Each act of cruelty or violence [or cheating] is somehow associated, harmonized, with every other act. Bad and mediocre people are tempted to sin by their own habitual weaknesses. The earlier lies or depths or adulteries make the next one that much easier to contemplate. Having already cut so many corners, the thinking goes, what's one more here or there. Why even aspire to virtues that you probably won't achieve when it's easier to remain the sinner that you already know yourself to be."

As a consequence of my time in the Holy Land, my skepticism about humankind continues, healthy and vibrant.

34
Endings Pitiful, Magnificent, Pathetic

*No one knows whether death is really the greatest blessing
a man can have,
but they fear it is the greatest curse, as if they knew well.*
—Plato

What do Elvis Presley, Bob Marley and Anastasio Somoza
have in common? Not much, except yours truly covered
their funerals. CBS sent me to so many interments that I
became an expert, even considered running for Vice
President of the United States.
Elvis came to rest at Graceland in Memphis. Marley was
put on view in Kingston. Somoza in Miami.

For those of you who are not conversant with your
dictators, Somoza was one of the last Caudillos, strong
men riding white horses, charging at windmills at every
turn. Fidel Castro fits that category as well. So why bury
Somoza in Miami? Simple. Sooner or later all Latin
American dictators, dead or alive, wind up in Miami.

Something tells me, however, Miami will not be the final
resting place for that Communist, Castro. Unless, of
course, someone wants to witness a monumental
graveyard desecration by south Florida's Cuban-American
exile community. You know how animated those Cubans
can be at the mere mention of El Comandante en Jefe. And
don't even whisper Elián González in their presence. Truth
be known, those anti-Castroites would use almost any
excuse to trample all over democracy. Talk about your
dictators.

Back in Memphis, Elvis was "straining at stool" when he died on August 16, 1977. That's how the medical examiner characterized the death of the king of rock 'n' roll. Morbidly obese and eating only toasted peanut butter and bacon sandwiches, Presley was found dead on his bathroom floor. His heart gave out when he was only 42. Presumably, the immediate cause of death was a heart attack brought on by a stressful attempt to void feces from his bowel. What a pitiful ending.

Cardiovascular problems ran in his family. Drugs ran in his bloodstream. All the king's horses and all the king's men couldn't put Presley together again. It took seven all-white limos and hearses and thousands of fans to honor and bury him. They came not to bury Presley but to praise him. A lot of them believe Elvis is alive still. But Elvis has left the building, for sure. Many of his devotees drove their cars thousands of miles, enduring self-imposed sleeplessness simply to be close to their sovereign's memorial service.

His followers besieged Elvis' Graceland mansion, where his body rested. The towering iron gates at the entrance crashed down as his disciples flung themselves in vain efforts to get in for a last look. A vanguard of police drove them back. Not many were able to join the endless line to pass by the coffin. Most were satisfied with merely showing up.
No pictures were allowed, no cameras permitted inside. But my artist did get in to sketch the dead royalty who was decked out in one of his colorful majestic uniforms. The artist had to sketch his remains from memory. Elvis' family would have thrown a fit and would have cast her out if they caught her with a sketch pad doodling his dead body. As it was, her artistic memory rendered the ruler in various shades of blue. Even the face of Elvis, perhaps fittingly, was blue. This had to have been the artist's blue period. How macabre, I thought, when I saw the weird

representation. But, left with no other video, I used the peculiar picture in my televised tribute to this authentic American idol.

Picture this: The CBS Evening News with Walter Cronkite did not lead with the news of the fallen American hero. The producers of the broadcast put my story in third place in the lineup. This failing by the aging Cronkite and his executive producer, Burton Benjamin, occurred because they were out of touch with the times. Elvis was not in their vocabulary. Critics let them know in no uncertain terms the producers had let down themselves and their audience by not topping the newscast with a bulletin about the death of the century. Chagrined, Cronkite and Benjamin owned up publicly to their mistake. They apologized.

The producers wouldn't get this one wrong. Last rites for Reggae luminary Bob Marley were accorded top billing. My own producer on this story, Joe Carroll, saw to that. In search of a local helper, we strolled through the billowing smoke of Kingston's main pastime—the inhaling of huge numbers of marijuana cigarettes. There is nothing scientific about it, just the simple suction of vaporized cannabinoids from small pipes, bongs, joints or blunts. Anything the locals could puff on for their eye-glazing highs. Marijuana and Bob Marley are synonymous. The cancer that got him was provoked, perhaps, by his perpetual intake of the grass. Malignant melanoma was the official cause of death. Elvis liked pain killers. Marley liked ganga. The stuff is just as much a part of Jamaican culture as cherry pie is to ours. Zombies patrol the streets of Kingston goaded by the eternal flame of hash.

A friend of mine who went on a trip in Jamaica recalled his sojourn with the funny weed. Speeding down a mountain road, his car nearly plunged into oblivion. He and his driver were under the influence, so to speak. The driver's brain was on cannabis-induced pause for precious seconds while

223

the car went on its merry way. Moments before there would have been a fatal plunge, the driver came to his senses and reminded himself out loud, "Pay attention! Pay attention! I'm driving." All survived without a scratch on their bodies. I can't say as much for their brains.

Marley's was a state funeral, a national wake. The mood, however, was somehow upbeat. His embalmed corpse lay in state in the National Arena in Kingston, the right hand clutching a copy of the King James Version of the Bible opened at Psalm 23, the left hand atop the strings of his red Gibson Les Paul guitar. Also in the casket was a stalk of marijuana placed there by his widow, Rita.

In Jamaica, everyone claimed to be Bob's friend. A policeman in uniform smoked a spliff and bemoaned the loss of Marley on his way to the memorial. A cab driver who professed to know him personally said he liked the Reggae King of the world because, "He smoked the herb of life."

The policeman and the cabman joined 100,000 others of the public allowed to file past the coffin to take a final look. Marley's head was covered with dreadlocks, but not his own. Chemotherapy to treat his cancer had left him baldheaded. A wig covered his bald skull. His dead eyes were shuttered and his ears were blind to the powerful public address system that blasted out his ultra-famous recordings. "Babylon system is a vampire," Bob's voice wailed as 6,000 chairs filled up with family, musicians, members of the government, and press. Seats were also reserved for the Twelve Tribes of Israel, a popular sub-sect of Rastafari founded in Jamaica in the late 1960s with whom Marley was closely associated.

The thousands gathered to praise Bob Marley profusely applauded former Jamaican Prime Minister Michael Manley as he entered the arena. Marley's followers in Jamaica, most oppressed for years, embraced Manley's pro-Cuban policies that eased their own pain. Marley's lyrics honoring the poor comforted them, too. But those words and Manley's socialist policies provoked the disastrous enmity of the United States government, which supported the conservative Edward Seaga as he deposed Manley to become Jamaica's new prime minister. Still, both men, current and former PMs, socialist and capitalist, shook hands and smiled in front of the Marley coffin and, at that moment, all Jamaicans seemed united in their humble regard for the fallen artist and his unique, off-beat artistry. Yet Manley, still a friend of the oppressed, was glad-handed by the crowd of mourners in stark contrast to the tepid approval granted Seaga, who hurried to his seat surrounded by uniformed guards.

In the end, they all sang together Elvis Presley's favorite hymn: "Then sings my soul, my Savior God, to thee/ How great Thou art, how great Thou art."

Maybe the other-world, marijuana-induced condition prompted Marley to write and sing so beautifully. Built into our funereal story for Cronkite was the famous Marley melody "No Woman no Cry." It makes me cry every time I hear it. Such sentimental drivel branded me on the day Marley's music died. It accosts me to this day. The genesis of that song is a secret unveiled to you now at this very moment. I have kept the secret for its sentimentality. "No Woman no Cry" was born on an airplane. Now you know the secret.

Marley was on a Boeing 747 to London when he reached into his sub-conscious revelry and pulled out a one-of-a-kind. The soaring lyric coupled with the unique off-beat syncopate produced a work never duplicated. His soul, the soul of Jamaica, was laid bare for all to see. And what they saw resonated with people all over the world who longed for justice. It gave voice to social misgivings in Jamaica and everywhere else—an anthem to global poverty and unfairness.

> …Good friends we have had, oh good friends we've lost …
> In this bright future you can't forget your past …
> Everything's gonna be alright …
> Don't cry women.

Marley sang that song for the first time in his brother's London apartment. At his funeral, the breadth of his appeal and his reach for justice united a myriad of people in attendance. Far right and far left politicians came together. Rich and poor joined to celebrate his life. A commonality raced through those who saluted him for his ability to access every stratum of society. Bob Marley brought out the best in everybody. What a magnificent ending.

Anastasio Somoza brought out the worst in everybody. There was nothing surprising about his burial. Fifty thousand mourners had attended his father's service, a state funeral, in Managua, Nicaragua, back in 1956. Dad was as tyrannical and corrupt as his son—maybe more so. Anyway, he was marked for assassination. So was Anastasio, Jr. The Somozas never learn.

Dad's assassin, Rigoberto Lopez Perez, a 27-year-old poet, killed the elder Somoza at a party in Leon, Nicaragua. Somoza had come to power after killing Augusto Sandino, the rebel leader whose name was taken by the Sandinistas who prevail in Managua to this day. Anastasio junior was a chip off the old block. His own brutal dynastic rule was punctuated daily with the killing and maiming of innocent civilians.

In 1979, Sandinista revolutionaries mounted attacks against the militarized Somoza family dictatorship in towns and cities all over the country. In fierce, bloody fighting the Sandinistas were on their way to overthrowing Samoza that year. Samoza's national guard hit back viciously. In the central city of Masaya, I saw Somoza's troops drag teenage boys from their homes and execute them on the spot. The blood-thirsty troopers went house-to-house bludgeoning people simply suspected of helping Sandinista rebels who plotted Somoza's downfall.

Lewis Bailey, my cameraman, and I barely escaped the gunfire turned on us for taking pictures of their viciousness. When my producer, Phil O'Connor, proposed cameraman Bailey and I penetrate even farther to get better pictures I demurred. Isn't that a lovely, polite way of saying *Hell no, I won't go!* That's exactly what I said. I told O'Connor that instead of going forward, I was taking the crew out of the battle. And that, my friends, was the better part of valor. We were pinned down for hours in Masaya not far from the burning bodies of their comrades. Hopped up on stimulants, the national guardsmen were savage. They had been on the run for days without sleep, putting down Sandinista uprisings all over the country.

Composed mainly of ignorant farm boys from the hinterland, Somoza's praetorian guard never numbered more than 800. They were poorly led, frightened and worn out schoolboys without any schooling. They shot people down like dogs and moved on. This indiscriminate murdering caused Somoza's inevitable end. Even U.S.-backing of the hideous ruler in the Nicaraguan civil war could not save Somoza, following a horrifying scene replayed on American television night after night.

On June 20, 1979, my colleague and fellow West Virginian Bill Stewart, an ABC correspondent covering the war, was shot dead by one of Somoza's guards. Stewart and his camera crew had driven their van to within several yards of a government outpost. Leaving his crew behind inside the van marked "foreign press," Stewart approached the outpost to get permission to cover some action.

His cameraman, unnoticed by a lieutenant manning the post, sensed something bad was about to happen. He focused on Stewart and began taking the footage that would change history in a flash. Stewart's interpreter, Juan Espinoza, walked ahead of him to explain their peaceful intentions. Then Stewart, who spoke no Spanish, approached. He held his press credentials in one hand and a white flag in the other and walked up to the guard. The sentry raised his rifle, and Stewart dropped to his knees. After motioning Bill to lie down, the guard kicked him in the side, then stood back, took aim and shot Stewart behind the ear. Espinosa was murdered seconds later. The entire scene was captured on the cameraman's videotape.

Somoza's goons tried to censor our reports but were fooled by ABC technicians responsible for sending out, via satellite, the pictures of Stewart's murder. The technicians slipped the incriminating video between other, relatively benign shots. Somoza tried to blame the shooting on the Sandinistas, but an uproar erupted in the U.S. as the awful shooting was broadcast coast-to-coast and around the world. That fueled outrage against the Nicaraguan government and caused the United States to withdraw its support of the Somoza regime.

The Somozas are yet another example of the sort of animals the U.S. supported in Latin America just because they were against Communism, Cuba and the Soviet Union. The U.S. supplied the guns that killed off Nicaraguan citizens who had done nothing but want to live. That is the mark of pragmatism, not greatness.

The Soviet Union was trying to project power into the Western Hemisphere through Cuba. So if it took Somoza and his thugs to stop the infiltration, so be it. Latin America was, of course, a battleground in the Cold War. Monroe Doctrine was in play. Enforce it at all costs!

In July 1979, Somoza fled before advancing Sandinista fighters could lynch him. Otherwise he might have faced the same kind of fate Libya's Muammar Gaddafi suffered in 2011, when Libyan revolutionaries beat and abused him and put a bullet in his brain following 42 years of dictatorial rule. Hatred toward the Nicaraguan despot was palpable, too.

Somoza slinked off to Miami, but President Carter ordered him out of the U.S. Paybacks are hell. Leaving, Somoza boarded a chartered yacht to vacation in the Caribbean. A shotgun could be seen in the pilothouse. Somoza, heavily armed, stayed below and out of sight of our prying eyes. In an unmemorable interview I had conducted with Somoza in Managua a few months before his finish there, he was fat and cheerful in his unearned military uniform. His personal masseuse had just completed a very hands-on massage. Somoza glared at me, then smiled and gave me a warning punch in the gut, clearly meaning don't mess with me. I got the message.

But in the end I got the last word. His story on Cronkite's show displayed the bully running on his private race track. As he strode out of sight I informed the TV audience he "was running for his life."

My statement was prophetic. Somoza got as far as Paraguay, another U.S.-backed dictatorship posing as a democracy. On September 17, 1980, a seven-person Sandinista commando team ambushed the 54-year-old

229

Somoza. Some accounts say "Operation Reptile" to assassinate Somoza was planned in Moscow with direct help from Fidel Castro. Somoza had left his exile estate in his Mercedes-Benz S-class sedan accompanied by his driver, Cesar Gallardo, and financial advisor, Jou Baittiner. A rocket propelled grenade slammed into the car, a direct hit. It exploded, killing Somoza and the other two instantly. Somoza's charred body was so unrecognizable that forensics had to identify him by using his unburned feet.

On September 20, 1980, Somoza was entombed in a Miami cemetery as thousands of his fellow exiles and supporters wept and screamed, "Viva Somoza."

A solemn prayer service for Somoza, whose family ruled Nicaragua with an iron fist for decades, was held in a chapel at the Caballero Funeral Home in the section of Miami known as Little Havana for its rabidly anti-Castro population of Cuban exiles. Somoza's mother, Salvadora, and his Florida-born wife, Hope, from whom he had been estranged, joined his namesake son, Anastasio, and four other children in attending the service.

It took the funeral cortege nearly two hours to travel the few short blocks to the cemetery because the very large crowd of mourners blocked the way, surrounding the hearse bearing Somoza's coffin.

An informal uniformed honor guard of Cuban veterans of the failed 1962 Bay of Pigs invasion walked alongside.

Two U.S. congressmen, Larry McDonald (D-GA) and John Murphy (D-NY) attended the services. McDonald inexplicably blamed President Carter for Somoza's assassination.

Some 15,000 countrymen, many of them once members of the Somoza-led Nicaraguan National Guard, fled with him to Miami and stayed after he left for Paraguay. Many feared for their future because their temporary U.S. visas were to expire, and most had blood on their hands. They, along with their Cuban-American benefactors and their despotic leader, were bound for history's dust bins. What a pathetic ending.

35
Get 'em In the Tent on Time

There's a Sucker Born Every Minute
–P. T. Barnum

Great TV anchors, like great carnival barkers, use many methods—some ethical, some not so ethical—to attract audiences. If they are truly successful, they can ensnare their spectators within the first fifteen seconds of their spiel. Otherwise, they run the risk of losing out altogether and of being exposed as the con artists they really are. I have seen anchor men and anchor women come and go like horses on a merry-go-round. Each time they came around, though, they were likely to be a horse of a different color.

The late Peter Jennings was like that. Jennings' classic good looks and reassuring presence made him a natural pick for the anchor's chair, even though he preferred reporting in the field. In 1965, ABC made him the anchor of the program *Peter Jennings with the News*, which ran opposite the shows of venerable newsmen like Walter Cronkite on CBS and David Brinkley on NBC. Jennings lasted two years in the role before quitting, ABC said, "…to become a foreign correspondent for the network."
Here's the truth. Jennings did not quit. ABC ousted him from his anchor chair because of poor ratings. His youth did not serve him well when, at age 25, he was up against Cronkite and Brinkley, men twice his age. Old school observers weren't ready for the young upstart. At the time age and experience counted for something.

When Jennings finally got some age on him and great experience to boot, he came roaring back to give Tom

Brokaw and Dan Rather a run for their money. Jennings was best known as the sole anchor of ABC's *World News Tonight* for 22 years. It took years for Jennings to reappear in the ABC anchor slot because years were required for the network watchers to appreciate his presentation. In that time, Rather replaced Cronkite, and Brokaw replaced Brinkley. By the beginning of the 21st century, Rather, Brokaw, Jennings and their fans were all on the same page.

The relationship was mutually beneficial; the network anchors gave their aficionados what they wanted to see and hear and, in return, the vast gallery of admirers handed them the ratings they required to stay on top. But ratings and celebrity do not give you the best information. The news, by definition, is reality not based on which anchor has the nicest smile or seems the best informed. Leave those criteria for stardom to entertainers, not news men and women.

Because the networks and cable TV have not kept entertainment and news gathering separate, what you see on TV is blurred. We are in the age of "infotainment," in which viewers cannot discern the difference between reality and fiction. Within this ambiance of mortal struggle for ratings and acceptance, news people will do almost anything to keep viewers happy. If they don't, they will be on the street and their employers, the owners of CBS, NBC, ABC and CNN will sell off, or dispose of, their news divisions much as they would get rid of an "unproductive" division that made toasters, for example.

So it is in the interest of the TV news anchors to be as attractive as possible while airing the most fantastic tales that have nothing to do with reality. Under pressure by their multi-national conglomerate bosses like GE and Disney and Viacom and Comcast and Time Warner, the highly promoted news stars have become celebrities in their own right. Like the late Andy Rooney of *60 Minutes* stardom, they may pretend publicly that they eschew their celebrity, but privately they glory in it. Foisting themselves off as the guardians of the First Amendment, they are, in fact, not much more than highly paid floggers of misinformation, pandering to the transitory and consumer-centric tastes of the people. TV news, therefore, is show biz, not to be taken seriously. That seems benign, not dangerous, until you explore the ramifications of it.

When anchors and their superiors abandon good journalism for the sake of ratings, viewers are shortchanged. Competition for eyeballs is so frenzied, and fear of winding up number three or four on the nightly totem-pole so intense, Rather and his compatriots at ABC and NBC embarrassed themselves in the fight. Their desire to scoop one-another was so severe that inevitable mistakes were made.

For instance, my old friend Rather committed a fatal error when he forced a story to air without sufficient investigation. He was afraid other news outlets known to be pursuing the story would break it before he did. After *60 Minutes II* ran his report about President George W. Bush's military record, numerous critics questioned the authenticity of the documents upon which the report was based. Rather subsequently admitted on air that the documents' authenticity could not be proved. Not only had Rather humiliated himself, he had mortified CBS. The Tiffany network and Rather came under attack from almost all quarters.

In the aftermath of the incident, CBS fired multiple members of the CBS News staff, but allowed Rather to stay on. He retired under pressure as the anchor of the *CBS Evening News* on March 9, 2005. At the end of Rather's time as anchor, the *Evening News* lagged behind the *NBC Nightly News* and *ABC World News Tonight* in the ratings. The avuncular former anchor Cronkite, whom Rather succeeded, said this about Rather: "It surprised quite a few people at CBS and elsewhere that, without being able to pull up the ratings beyond third in a three-man field, that they tolerated his being there for so long."

Let's be clear. Ratings equal money. The higher the ratings, the bigger the payday. Networks lose hundreds of millions of advertising dollars when the ratings drop or fail to meet expectations. So the Brian Williamses and the Katie Courics and the Wolf Blitzers are worth millions to the networks as long as they can pull in viewers. Like NBA and NFL stars, network anchors are rewarded with multi-million-dollar contracts. Just like film idol George Clooney, they have agents who negotiate their business agreements. Makeup artists attend to them. Costume designers dress them. Lighting technicians put them in the best light. Producers and writers do most of the heavy lifting. All they have to do is show up for work and not stumble. But if they stumble, they're out. No matter that they may be excellent reporters. Their main job is pleasing the public, not piercing the places of safety where evil may hide.

Such a system destroys good reporters. It makes a mockery of professional journalism. It places high value on cosmetics. It insults the intelligence of the viewing audience. And it does so without remorse. Those journalists who don't mind prostituting themselves reinvent their lives to satisfy the demands of their profession. They transform from the healthy transparency of open-mindedness to the perverted loudspeakers of ignorance and fetid alarm. Instead of informing their reader with honest intelligent insight, they appeal to the lowest common denominator with a vengeance.

In pursuing news stories, the story should not be about the pursuer. Air time is wasted by putting reporters on the air instead of the story itself. In these days of celebrity correspondents, you can't know whether a headline is for real, because the reporter invariably gets in the way.
In addition, "talking heads" take up enormous slices of the little time the big three networks devote to news these days. On cable TV news, to fill up the 24-hour news cycle, almost all of what you see on the screen is yammering heads. And all too frequently the heads know absolutely nothing about the facts. Far too often they simply make it up. Airing a talking head is much cheaper to do than actually exploring the events and people who constitute the real news. Putting a face on TV is much easier and quicker than committing hours and days and sweat and questioning required to tell the truth. Because audiences demand instant gratification, the so-called news outlets are more than willing to fulfill their needs by going on air instantly with someone who acts as if he knows what he is talking about.

Case in point: Remember when four school children and their teacher were killed in their school yard by a couple of their classmates in Jonesboro, Arkansas, back in 1998? Ten other kids were wounded in the shooting. I was on duty in the NBC Atlanta bureau that March day when the shooting occurred. Highly skilled bureau technicians beseeched their satellites for pictures of the schoolhouse madness. Tom Brokaw's deadline was just minutes away, no time to send a correspondent from Atlanta to Jonesboro to sort out the insane situation.

I read accounts of the murders as written by local wire reporters who could or could not be trusted to provide veracity. I had to take their word for it. Then I looked at the satellite pictures taken by local photographers who could or could not be trusted. I had to take their video for certainty. I then synthesized wire reports and satellite photos into a two-minute story for *The NBC Nightly News.* I wrote and narrated the whole thing as if I were an authority. I was guessing the whole time. But the story went on the air with my name on it as if I knew who, what, when, where and how it all went down in Jonesboro.

Adding insult to injury, I let Delta fly me to Jonesboro to catch up. I never caught up. A limo whisked me to a satellite "uplink" truck for a "live" report just down the street from the spotlighted school. I never got to the school, mind you. I never spoke to anybody who had been to the school. I never interviewed any classmates or teachers or police or first-responders, not anybody. NBC was too eager to get me on the air first with the latest than to allow me to do the legwork any reporter worth his salt must do to get it right. Time would not allow such painstaking drudgery. Without too much protest, I was hooked up to a live camera for the on-the-scene, breathless report I was supposed to deliver. I gave them what I knew for sure, which wasn't much. I never was very good at lying.

I told you watching TV news these days could be hazardous to your mental health. You are being misled by performers posing as Edward R. Murrow as they act out important scenes of our time with great solemnity. I'm warning you. Don't believe them.

If you need more evidence, I am glad to provide it. For illustration I shall recall for you a typical episode in which anchors take stories away from reporters under their command. The syndrome is called big-footing in the industry. After reporters unearth a really important news story, the big footer steals it to enhance his own reputation. Big Foot may go to the scene of the report and push the lowly reporter aside and put his brand on it. The disorder is sort of like someone stealing another person's invention and making a fortune off it.

Tom Brokaw big-footed me in Birmingham, Alabama. On April 8, 1998, an F5 tornado hit Birmingham communities, killing 32 people. I rushed in for NBC News and properly covered the developing story. In early afternoon, I discovered a man and woman stumbling around in what turned out to be their churchyard. But the church was nowhere to be seen. It had been completely obliterated by the tornado, wiped off the face of the earth. Only the concrete slab on which the church had been founded—only that slab and the church entrance sign—remained.

The couple I had found told me a horrifying story about how they had come to the scene to determine whether anything remained, and they were in shock. Not only because their church was history, but because a premonition had come true. You see, ordinarily the church would have been packed with congregants attending the Wednesday night prayer meeting. But just hours before the tornado hit town, even before alerts and predictions the wind storm was on its way, their minister had had a premonition. Somehow he knew trouble was brewing. He had telephoned each of the parishioners to tell them he was canceling the prayer meeting and they should stay at home. The church doors were locked because all had been turned away by the preacher's warning. No member of the flock was injured or killed that terrible night.

In addition to the interview with the despondent couple, I, of course, wanted to interview their savior, their prophetic preacher. But he was not reachable because he was out and about tending to his churchly duties. No cellphones back then. Time was short, deadline approaching rapidly. I assembled my story and fed it to New York where mine was the lead report on Brokaw's *Nightly News* that night, even without the crucial interview with the minister. No problem, I thought. I would catch up with the minister and interview him sooner or later. And what a story that would be. Brokaw must have thought the same thing. He jumped in immediately, ordering his producers to find the preacher so he could do the award-winning interview and follow up report for his broadcast the next night. I was dismissed without fanfare and told I could be on my way. Brokaw would handle it. And he did. The story was spectacular.

He soared to pen *The Greatest Generation.* He nose-dived to interfere in Birmingham. Kudos to Brokaw. As petty as that episode may seem to you, it is still a good example of "Big Foot." Moreover, it is a luminous insight into the triviality of the news business wherein big people stoop so low for their own good. It conjures the perfect cliché in which a high powered Katherine Parker (Sigourney Weaver) steals a blockbuster idea from her secretary, Tess McGill (Melanie Griffith) in *Working Girl.*

The charlatans are really good at what they do. Above all, they have their own careers, not your need to know, at the middle of their self-absorption. Dan Rather went to Afghanistan and cross-dressed like a member of the Mujahadeen, not for self-protection, but for self-promotion. "Gunga Dan," as the funny papers dubbed him, received a lot of attention for that news stunt. Some people thought he was crazy. But they spelled his name correctly.

Bill O'Reilly wasn't always the TV superstar of America's right wing. In the beginning he did not exalt himself to rake in millions of dollars. He was a lowly cub reporter for CBS in Atlanta earning regular wages when I knew him. I could tell he never liked being truthful. It's hard work to set aside your prejudices and ferret out the truth even if the truth upsets you. No, Mr. O'Reilly couldn't take it. He was terribly vexed when awakened in the middle of the night by the news desk and ordered out in the cold darkness to do yeoman chores. That was beneath him. He left CBS News following a petty spat with Bob Schieffer because Bob had used some uncredited video O'Reilly's camera crew had shot. Congratulations, Bill, for your successful career as a mouthpiece for extremists.

My good friend and crafty huckster of right wing nonsense, Bernard Goldberg, fell into the trap of self-aggrandizement a few years ago. Bernie was one of the most promising of all the producer/reporters at *CBS News* when CBS News was CBS *News*. In our 20s, we were pals, stalking evil and exposing ignorance every chance we had. He was my producer *par excellance*. Bernie hated slight-of-hand characters and misleaders. Liars and deceivers were on his hit list. There was hell to pay if you tried to hoodwink him. If you succeeded in sending him off on a wild-goose chase, he fired at you without warning.

I'll never forget the time Zeke Segal sent Bernie off to a non-story in Miami. Bernie detested non-stories. They were a waste of his precious time. Segal was the CBS bureau chief in Atlanta, noted for using work as a pastime. One night about 2 a.m., our cameraman, Roger Conner, was shaken from sleep by a Zeke alarm bell: "Hey, Roger, go to Welch!" Click ... Puzzled and staggering about in semi-slumber, Roger made airline reservations to Wales. Roger thought Zeke had ordered him to film a story in Wales, thousands of miles away. Double-checking from Miami before boarding his flight to Wales, Roger phoned the bureau to learn that Wales was not his destination. It was Welch! Welch, West Virginia—something to do with mining, coal mining.

Anyway, Bernie was livid when he returned to the bureau from a long and fruitless journey to Miami. He was right in Zeke's face, not three inches away from Zeke's wide eyes. I don't know how Bernie kept from bursting out in laughter. Zeke's eyes, each on its own, went East and West at the same time. You never knew whether he was looking at you or at some passing skirt. In addition to being a deceiver, Zeke was a skirt chaser. And a Marty Feldman lookalike. But there I go again, off the subject. Bernie screamed, "Zeke, it will have to be snowing in Miami before I make another trip down there for you."

The very next morning Bernie received a call at home from Zeke. "Hey, Bernie," Zeke sniggered. "Go to Miami. It's blanketed in the white stuff, hah, hah, hah." You guessed it. Snow had fallen overnight in Miami, the first snowfall down there in a hundred years. And that was a story Bernie could not refuse.

The hard worker in that bureau was Bernie Goldberg. I always admired him for his tenacity in his objective search for reality. I wouldn't have called him a liberal—nor a conservative. Bernie was a humanitarian without any humanity—a straight shooter who glorified himself by always turning an honest phrase for fidelity. I could never have imagined him writing that paltry little tome he titled *Bias*.

That *New York Times* best seller exposed Bernie as a narrow-minded drum major for lost causes. I was astonished by his emergence as a subjective little man dedicated to gross overstatements and pathetic neo-conservative rhetoric. That wasn't the Bernie Goldberg I had known. The Bernie I knew would not permit a George Wallace to get away with outrageous absurdities. There was no room in that Bernie's lexicon for the vile, indecent orations of the ignorant. He never subscribed to the magazines of hate and intolerance. So what on earth prompted him to go over to the dark side? Had he lost his mind? Or maybe he had misplaced his moral compass.

Bernie and I were big stars at CBS. He appeared frequently on Dan Rather's *Evening News.* So did I. Bernie's hallmark was a brilliant ability to produce news pieces that were distinctive, unique, out of the ordinary. The little guys became heroes in his stories. Big guys, the wealthy without portfolio, for example, were pilloried *sans* mercy. The very big shots he's in bed with these days were the detritus of Bernie's good old days. On one of those days Bernie snapped. He self-destructed. He signed his own death warrant in Dan Rather's newsroom.

After flying high for years with Rather, Bernie's days as one of Dan's boys were over. He was out. When it was all over, there was no snatching back the February 1996 scathing op-ed piece on media bias Bernie wrote in *The Wall Street Journal* titled "Networks Need a Reality Check: A firsthand account of liberal bias at CBS News." The article pummeled the man whose ring and other anatomical parts he had to kiss to get on the air. Dan would never again permit Bernie on *The Evening News*, for he had committed the unpardonable sin. He had double-crossed Dan the Man. Bernie had gone out of his way on the road to perdition, burrowing himself into the infinite hole of noncompliance. He had dug his own grave and seemed delighted to sleep in it; there was no coming back. And therein rests the real reason for Bernie's sudden shift.

I think he simply got tired of kowtowing and wanted to take his leave. It was not in Bernie's nature to be subservient. He had had it with Dan the Man. The romance was over. Honeymooning on West 57th Street, dancing with daddy, being a masseur to the star rubbed Goldberg the wrong way. Inventing *Bias* was inspired. Bernie could have walked out without motive, but he never did anything without motivation. What better way to incite divorce than getting caught with your *Bias* down.

Machiavellian to the core, plaintiff Goldberg served the divorce papers on defendant Rather in the op-ed piece that charged liberal bias in the media. And he got what he wanted—the instant ignition of Dan Rather's white hot temper—which burned Bernie's bridges at CBS forevermore. Laughing all the way to the bank with his best seller in hand, Bernie also outfoxed Fox in his bargain with the devil. He barreled away from sincerity, taking the low road because the high road was blocked.

How he must have gloried in writing the most memorable of his less than memorable sentences—something like, "If CBS News were a prison, many of its employees would be Rather's bitches." I told you I couldn't remember it exactly. What I do recall is this: It was the kind of rubbish you write when launching a new career that insults your friends and colleagues.

As with Bill O'Reilly before him, Goldberg reinvented himself, distorting a rather honorable sort into a mean-spirited backwoodsman. His timing was perfect. The conservative allegory was on the rise again in America. Bernie would fit right in. He had a brand new audience, including President Bush, who cravenly carried Bernie's book in public for show. He was in precise position to palm himself off as a savior of the notion that unwillingness or slowness to accept change or new ideas is a virtue. Barry Goldwater had espoused Bernie's view years earlier when he said, "Extremism in defense of liberty is no vice." Goldberg and Goldwater are angelic twins, a perfect law firm. And we all know what happened to Goldwater.

By the way, I don't think the news media are liberal-centric. Nor do I think they are conservative-centric. I think they are ego-centric. Of course Fox News isn't even part of what's left of respectable media. Neither is MSNBC. Both of those loudspeakers for political causes are exactly what they are:

Platforms for pretense, stages for sham, and playhouses for pomposity. Don't give them a second thought.

Ironically, the man who ousted Goldberg would, himself, be thrown out by CBS. Rather had so alienated himself at CBS, so inflated himself that he couldn't be taken seriously anymore. He was the 800-pound gorilla who had lost a lot of weight. His secretary told me Rather often would talk about himself in the third person during office discussions. "What are they saying about Rather today?" he would ask her.

I got caught in the middle of one of Rather's power plays. Rather had adopted me as one of his favorites, just like Goldberg. But so had the late Robert J. "Shad" Northschield, creator and executive producer of the iconic *CBS Sunday Morning with Charles Kuralt.* Northschield's ego was almost as large as Rather's. You didn't want to get caught in the middle of their dueling egos. I barely got out.

When Northschield tapped me to work for him full time on *Sunday Morning*, Rather went ballistic. Northschield was fond of my ability to apply the common touch when doing stories for his unique program. So was Rather. One would think being fought for by two important personages is a good thing. And one would be wrong. When tied at midpoint in the tug of war by two giants, the possibility of being torn apart is quite real. At the end of the day, though, the two apparently decided the war, and I, were simply not worth it. A peace treaty was signed. It accorded both warriors the right to use me whenever they wished. My workload would be doubled, but my pay check would stay the same. Such a deal!

There is no purity in news gathering and reporting. Not when reporters are pinning their own survival on a newsroom defined by commercial success. If the demand for a winning fourth quarter is the all-pervading goal of those who finance the news operations, the independence of those operations is compromised. If the pressure on news producers to come up consistently with stories that appeal to the popular inclinations of the public as opposed to the detached scrutiny of society, there cannot be a bold adherence to the grand idea of a free press.

Internal skirmishes among and between on-air and back scene superstars do not a sober news broadcast make. And when those skirmishes become the stuff of tabloid journalism, the misconduct is even more severe. Airing the dirty laundry of celebrity should be left to shows like *Entertainment Tonight.* When the peccadilloes of a Dan Rather become a headline in the *New York Times,* all reports and all reporters suffer. When reporters go off the grid to make themselves the center of attention, their primary responsibility to their readers and viewers is lost. Of course, the current heated environment in which the cult of the personality is celebrated only encourages bad behavior by would-be reporters. Getting their names in the newspapers and on TV should not trump getting the story and getting it right.

That old Communist Castro understood as well as anyone the smutty competitiveness in our industry. He knew every one of us would kill to get an on-camera interview with him. And he played his knowledge of our resolve to the hilt. In his olive greens and combat boots, the pistol toting, cigar smoking, international gangster was larger than life. By stroking his beard and caressing our egos he could get anything he wanted from us. He was a character made for television, and he knew it.

I know he chortled when Dan Rather engaged in specialized fisticuffs with Barbara Walters as they strenuously vied for his attention. Fidel impudently toyed with Diane Sawyer in her ardent quest to be his interrogator. He played all of us like a piano. He left the BBC sitting in a Havana hotel room for a year without ever making good on his promise to permit a sit down with him. The BBC even made a documentary film about the holdup called *Waiting for Fidel.*

Once the Rathers and the Walterses and the Sawyers leapt into Fidel's web, he bamboozled them all with his gratuitous pabulum. He could have read the Manhattan phone directory for them and they would have gone away satisfied. If he had wanted to, he could have written a best seller on how to fool the press. In fact, when he was in the Sierra Maestra making war on Batista, he sat for interviews while his men marched in the background. By the time the interview finished, the reporter thought thousands of Fidel's avid revolutionaries were in camp. In reality, Castro never had more than 120 soldiers in all. He simply marched the same soldiers back and forth to make the reporters think he was leading a mighty band of warriors.

The upshot: we helped win the revolution for Castro, and we kept it going for him. Edward R. Murrow did a long distance, live interview with a triumphant Castro following his victorious march into Havana in 1959. Even the great Murrow was taken in by the grand master of the media when Fidel solemnly announced on Murrow's *See It Now* that he was not a Communist. Shortly thereafter, Castro confiscated American-owned property on the island and played cozy-up with the Soviets, permitting Khrushchev to place strategic nuclear missiles just 90-miles from the U.S. mainland. No cameras allowed on that little ploy.

The TV networks for whom the news stars work must share the blame, of course, for allowing the folly that promotes the agendas of tyrants and other twisters of truth. There are ways to expose villains for what they are without muddying up the matter with the mugs of TV news superstars. A lot more would be revealed by simply taking the news personalities out of the equation.

A well-defined line ought to be drawn between those who profit from news divisions and the news managers, producers and reporters responsible for keeping the news divisions running. Emphasis on profit cannot and should not be the arbiter in the news industry. Not that there is anything wrong with profit. But the production of news and the production of toasters are two different matters. Toasters can be done without.

A free and independent press is fundamental to our nation, the lifeblood of democracy. It cannot and should not be dispensed with easily. But when it is in the hands of corporate bosses, the news media are liable to be corrupted by the drive for tangible yield. Shareholders despise companies that do not return a decent dividend. In this instance, though, the reward ought to be the support and furtherance of the American ideal of independent and honest debate.

If the debate steps on the toes of wrongdoers, so be it. Stepping on toes ought to be the highest objective, not a preoccupation with Hollywood. A devastating flood, not a reporter's ability to wade into the floodwaters for an exciting on-camera shot, should be the focus. For some reason, such shots appeal to viewers who look for common disaster instead of exerting the mental labor required in parsing a complex governmental issue. News experts entrusted with the valuable assets of objectivity and fairness need to be about the business of presenting the news, not the hucksterism of the carnival.

Clearly, ownership has the pivotal role in guaranteeing what you see and hear on TV reinforces your Constitutional guarantee of fair and accurate information, not a promise of comedic diversion. Big corporations with big pocketbooks now possess your access to news. Furthermore, they are the determiners of what you see and hear and read. And they cannot be trusted. Theirs is the behavior of marketplace chaos, not the guardian of integrity.

If they are not willing, or are unable, to abandon their robotic chase for revenue, they have no business being in charge of your newsrooms. If they are not capable of protecting the sacred covenant assured by the Founding Fathers, they have no right to control mass communications. If they continue to intimidate news producers by demanding top ratings instead of top thoughtfulness, they should give back the keys to the people's right to know.

These arguments are neither furtive nor perfidious. They have nothing to do with grandstanding. A soapbox is not the platform on which I take this stand, for it is out of a keen desire to inform about the dangers of inaction that provoke my words of caution. Do not misunderstand me. I have no ax to grind. Underestimating the potential for harm to our greatest institution by mindless business leaders is an obvious crime, not simply the worry of an armchair war correspondent.

A not so subtle affirmation of my diatribe can be seen in the appearance and attitude of the so-called newsmakers who are sought to go on news broadcasts. Victims are blond with blue eyes. Villains are cold, calculating and articulate. Don't expect to see stumbling, bearded, toothless people on the screen. Don't expect to see a shy, introverted, soft-spoken businessman or career woman on *60 Minutes* even if he or she ripped off a workingman or denied someone his civil rights. That offensive tycoon Donald Trump will get on the air for his shock value alone. Hell, he even has his own show. See what I mean?

Instead of selecting a person for air whose story alone is the criterion, show producers go for the most likeable or most hateable every time. That's show biz. To be sure they don't make a mistake the producers pre-interview their newsmakers to determine whether the subject is airworthy. As a result, would-be talking heads and politicians warp themselves into something they are not in order to fit the producer's whim. It ought to be the other way around. But it isn't.

 Abraham Lincoln wouldn't stand a chance these days. After all, who would put on the tube a guy with a stovepipe hat, an ominous visage, elephant ears, pasty skin, a huge face mole and a screechy voice? Wait a minute! They put me on the news, didn't they? "There it is," as my Vietnam era buddies would say.
Congressmen and congresswomen and presidents and their corporate buddies are all bunking in the same bed. Politicians depend on the media for air time and, by extension, for votes of the electorate. So they are not about to take on ABC's Disney, for example, to set things right.

The creation of an independent entity to own and operate a truly free press is not a task for the timorous. This idea is dynamite. But there must be a solution to the growing and perilous influence private owners foist on this very public of all our institutions. Something has got to change. If not, you are liable to be misled at least, betrayed at worst.

From the racial wars in America's south,
I became a war correspondent in 1970 in
America's first television war.
For 13 months in Vietnam,
I thought, like any other 31-
year-old, that I was bulletproof.
Here in Quang Tri, South Vietnam, I came face-to-face
with the horror at an Army Mobile Surgical Hospital (MASH).

My Vietnamese camera crew, local Vietnamese Army
troopers and I stood at attention
for the camera. Mr. Hai, in sunglasses, protected me even though I
towered over the diminutive Vietnamese.

U.S. Army medevac helicopters delivered dead and wounded GIs
to the MASH at Quang Tri. Young U.S. Army nurses scampered
from a South China Sea beach nearby the hospital to attend the
suffering soldiers. "...a scary deliveryman invariably swooped down
upon them and transfixed them with his cargo of the dead and badly
wounded. The beach goers scattered like a flock of seabirds frightened
into frenzied flight. The flap, flap, flap of helicopter blades beat down
upon them, urging them away from their sandy fantasy and into their
real world of blood bags and drip tubes.
Once again their escape plan had been foiled."

December 1993 - Questioning Les Aspin
in the halls of the Pentagon over his refusal to supply Americans
with armor in Somalia. He resigned shortly thereafter.

Army commanders were furious with me for showing a 2-second shot on NBC Nightly News of an American GI being dragged through the streets of Mogadishu, Somalia. Nineteen Americans and 1000 Somalis were killed during the Battle of Mogadishu on October 3, 1993. The debacle led to the resignation of Les Aspin as Defense Secretary.

On a military flight to Somalia with
Joint Chiefs Chairman General John Shalikashvili.
U.S. troops would be withdrawn from Somalia, in part, because
Shalikashvili's commanders said
"Real men don't do MOOTWA"—Missions Other Than War.
The mission in Somalia was a MOOTWA.

November, 1993—Shooting questions at Hillary Clinton, General Shalikashvili and Les Aspin on the steps of the Pentagon. There were few answers.

In 1995 covering the 72-hour operation
by American and Italian forces
to escort the last United Nations troops safely out of Somalia
that went off without any American casualties.
But as the last troops left, the U.S. Marines opened up with
several fusillades of machine-gun and cannon fire
as Somalis tried to enter the narrow American zone.

The military operation to evacuate the UN peace-keepers from Somalia complete, I got out without a scratch, always an objective of any sane correspondent.

More bodies, this time in Iran. Iran's Revolutionary Guards
savaged the dead Iraqi military helicopter pilots they had shot down
on a snowy mountaintop overlooking Kerkuk
in the semi-autonomous Kurdistan.

After we witnessed the aftermath of the Iranian military massacre
of the Iraqis during the eight-year Iran-Iraq war,
my producer and I were escorted back to Tehran
by Iran's Revolutionary Guards. The Guards, who'd once held
American diplomats hostage for 444 days,
asked us if we wanted cookies.
I was shocked, but the AK-47-toting Guards
smiled and bought cookies for us in Tabriz,
sweet medallions that melted in the mouth
taken from boxes wrapped in pretty pink ribbons.

During the Cold War, Fidel Castro and I had our differences
but he always astonished me with how well read he was
and how politically knowledgeable he could be.
His revolution was upset when the Soviet Union withdrew $5 billion
in annual assistance that kept Cuba afloat.
I told Fidel he should step down as president. He did so in 2008.

Castro continued to thumb his nose at the U.S. throughout
his nearly 50-year-long rule. He was a thorn in America's pride.
He and I agreed that the hostile U.S. foreign policy toward Cuba was
really a policy aimed at placating anti- Castro Cubans in Miami.
Republicans and Democrats alike demonized Castro to ensure,
cravenly, they could count on the formidable Cuban-American vote.

Cuban diplomat to the United States, Jose Ponce,
(2nd from right, front row) joined me and my closest friends at
croquet at my Great Falls, Virginia, home. Ponce apparently took
me seriously when I responded to his question about how Cuba
should react to illegal over flights of his country by anti-Castro,
Cuban-American pilots. Frivolously, I told him to "shoot them down."
Later, a Cuban MiG shot down two planes from Miami, killing four
and inviting international condemnation.

Cuban special forces troops preparing for a U.S. invasion
of the island after the shoot-down.
These photos were taken by me at a super-secret
Cuban special forces training center in the province
of Pinar del Rio, Cuba.

259

Posing with Cuban Special Forces commanders
at secret base in Pinar del Rio, Cuba.

Doing a "stand-upper" at the U.S. Naval Base
at Guantanamo Bay, Cuba. Leased from Cuba before Fidel Castro's
revolution, the base is isolated from the rest of Cuba by a mine field and
high fences. Heavily armed Cuban soldiers face their heavily armed U.S.
Marine "mirrors" in guard towers along the fence line. The base is used
today to house and interrogate terrorists following the 9/11 attacks.

At Patuxent River Naval Air Station in full oxygen mask array
preparing to fly a jet fighter mission off an aircraft carrier.
Cuba is only four minutes away by supersonic fighter from
Key West Naval air base.

Laotian hotelier Maurice Cavaliere was like a Graham Greene
character for sure. He and his plucky daughter, Danielle,
were my Intel agents, moneychangers and more when I covered
the extended Vietnam War in Laos in 1973. With close ties to the CIA,
the Laotian King, the Laotian Communists and other players
in the Southeast Asia conflict, Maurice and Danielle saved my
reporter life and became good friends.

Communism was everywhere in Huế, Vietnam's old Imperial capital, when I went back there for the 25th anniversary of the Tết offensive of 1968. At least fifty-seven thousand Americans died in combat during the Vietnam War which was lost to the communists. Today the U.S. has normal diplomatic and trade relations with a thriving, unified, communist Vietnam.

In Communist China's Tiananmen Square, a large city square in the center of Beijing, China, named after the Tiananmen Gate (Gate of Heavenly Peace) located to its North, separating it from the Forbidden City. In 2011, 1,344,130,000 were under communist rule in China. Today the U.S. has normal diplomatic and trade relations with Beijing.

American businessman supervising Chinese workers at a camera
production facility in Beijing.

My beloved 42' Grand Banks Trawler docked in Miami, Florida.
I lived aboard the boat when not covering Cuba and guerilla wars
in Central America. NBC Miami bureau chief Don Browne (in hat)
and I standing off the port bow.

Home sweet home in Great Falls, Virginia.
I got home once in a blue moon.

Rudi and Ray J welcome their daddy home in
Great Falls at Christmastime.

My best buddies, (above right) the late Harry Wiles and
(below) Saddam Hussein look-alike Doug Frost.
They possess secrets they've sworn never to reveal.

Saddam Hussein look-alike Doug Frost.

In July, 2012 my high school classmates and I
celebrated our 55th reunion. The celebration was held
in our high school hometown, St. Albans, West Virginia.
I am living not far away in Alum Creek, West Virginia where
I've folded myself up in my Rabel Mountain Roots.

VI
Country Roads

36
Finding A Way to Go Home

And he'd come home again to find it more
Desirable than it ever was before
How right it seemed that he should reach the span
Of comfortable years allowed to man!
—Seigfried Sassoon

By this time you have discerned that my climb into the heady stratosphere of freedom to report the truth— mountaineering there from state-sanctioned backwardness in West Virginia— was not all sweet tea and hush puppies. You will have noted, already, that the pitfalls were huge and uncountable. To be successful, my devotion to my work had to be focused like a laser beam. The unmitigated requirements imposed by CBS News left no room for a normal personal life. A commitment to such work meant a divorce from birthdays, anniversaries, home life and the like. All personal plans were put on hold, all vacations were cancelled, and all dinner parties put off. "Honey, I'm home," was never an everyday ritual. "Honey, I won't be home," was more like it.

More than anything else, my gritty determination to achieve upward mobility left little time for marital bliss. You always pay the price for craving more than the status quo. Twice divorced is twice honored, I always say. I had paid the price of ambition, and I began to think of returning home to the country roads of my youth.

Contemplating a way to go home, reverie pitched itself upon me more than ever before. Musing about history requires more than chronology. The entrails twist and turn

268

to reveal pathways of life foresworn and other roads often taken with abandonment and with outcome not questioned. So let's straighten it out. As with you or anyone who takes time to look inside oneself from time to time, to be introspective as they say, a review is absolutely necessary. Along the way one thing was always certain. I would return. I would go back because the strength and honor picked up originally in my ancestries, the courage that sustained me along the way remains in the mountains, still. So I wanted to soak it up anew. I wanted to be sure of it so the meaning of the long roadway to my ending is not bargained away. In returning home, I believed, I would reassure myself that I had not lost my way.

I must consider how I got to this point. After 20 years with CBS and 13 years with NBC, I came to realize I was getting less air time, and one of the reasons I was not showing up as much on that little screen in your living room had to do with the way I looked. I had grown too old to present the youthful visage required of everyone on TV except for those chosen few such as Andy Rooney and Mike Wallace, who were coveted for their wrinkles and weighty persona. I left on my own terms, getting out before I was forced out. Even then, though I felt the tug of the mountains, I chose other paths for a while.

I had spent four years at the Pentagon as the national security correspondent for NBC from 1993 to 1997, and from 1997 through 1998, I was NBC's Cuba expert, having reported on 150 different visits to that "imprisoned" island beginning in 1975. Based in part on that résumé, the CIA offered me a job directly after my leave-taking from the visible role I had enjoyed on TV for 43 years. I went to work for a CIA-oriented organization called Business Executives for National Security. After the second Gulf War I became a contractor for the Defense Department, setting up a new television network, and at about the same time I was employed by another defense related company called the Rendon Group in D.C. The mountains' magnetic pull grew in my heart, but still I stayed in exile, working as a crisis communications expert for another D.C. outfit.

For seven years beginning in 2004 I shuttled between Washington, D.C. and West Virginia, after accepting employment with the University of Charleston. (Remember, that's West Virginia, not South Carolina.) During those years I also served as a teacher and consultant at a prep school in Ohio. I returned for good in 2011 after 45 years of self-imposed exile. Throughout my life I have experienced cultural diversity, traveling from the world of mountain hollows to dwell on the planet of gleaming cities, taking up residency in New York, Washington, Miami, Atlanta, Dallas, Cleveland, Saigon and Tel Aviv.

I was born in Kanawha County and reared not far from my relatives on Rabel Mountain, where only mountain people, my people, have lived for generations.

West Virginia is now and forever more my home, but I continue to sally forth for interesting assignments. In June 2012, I went to Cuba to set up a journalism course for students at Washington State University's Edward R. Murrow College of Communications, where I am an adjunct professor.

37
Transition

I will lift up mine eyes unto the hills,
from whence cometh my help.
My help cometh from the Lord
—Psalms 121:1-2

I am not idle, yet I have ample time to roam the mountains of home. There is a grounding of the soul in origination. Each day big feet now walk in the same mud where my little feet played, conjuring a renewal of the appetites of life. Taking in the landscape of my originality, especially along the highways and byways little changed in these mountains, refreshes my affirmation that what I did in returning to the hills was the right thing to do. Most other emigrants remain in exile, but I am instructed by the poverty of the hills that expelled me. The acceptance I rejected in my getting away, I now see as a kind of solace for the common folk. After all, how can the grievances of the outer realm befall anyone closed up in the never-changing, self-imposed comfort of home? In walking the wastelands of West Virginia, though, I am reminded endlessly that constancy in nostalgia is a formula for disaster. Refusal to wake up to and enter into the modern world while basking in tried and true religiosity will have a very bad ending. I feel compelled to do something about this inordinate capacity to cling to the past.

The transition from 24/7 to "maybe next week," though, is hard. I struggle to find a balance between knowing what I know to be true on the planet of ideas with listening to the meanderings of a backwoods populace so sure there is no verity beyond grandfather's accuracy. It's tough sledding.

271

To my neighbors, wars and rumors of wars, both military and social, are theories to be prayed away and nothing more. Global warming is a myth among my fellow citizens who dismiss the very real danger as something made up by Al Gore, their nemesis. The Environmental Protection Agency is a Communist conspiracy out to destroy the coal industry on which the populace has pinned its hopes for generations despite unambiguous warnings about the industry's imminent demise. Only about 20,000 miners are at work today in West Virginia compared with 126,000 in 1948. Wal-mart, not coal mining, is the biggest private employer in the state.

Fifty-five outmoded and lethargic county governments serve poorly West Virginia's declining population, when 14 streamlined and modernized shires would do. Although each county has a board of education, West Virginia ranks 47th nationally in educating its youth.

A crumbling road system cited for one of the highest highway death rates in the nation continues to bedevil residents and turn away potential industries that require first-rate roadways to both import raw materials and export their products. The isolation that is so soothing for so many here for so long is not a tonic. It is a cancer that is killing its host.

As I tread the mountains of home, I reflect on West Virginia and her place in the nation. My home state is a woebegone corner of the United States. In 1863, Abraham Lincoln granted statehood to stubborn mountain people in western Virginia to spite those in eastern Virginia who had seceded from the Union. The division rewarded those Virginians who stuck with the Union and punished those who followed General Robert E. Lee.

It was surprising when religiously fundamental voters in West Virginia gave the Catholic, John F. Kennedy, a stunning victory over Hubert Humphrey in the 1960 Democratic primary. Handing victory to a Catholic in religiously diffident West Virginia was totally unpredictable—a stunning event that propelled Kennedy into the national limelight as a winner despite his religion.

I was still in West Virginia in 1963 when John F. Kennedy came to the state to thank West Virginians for propelling him into the presidency. It was exactly one hundred years after West Virginia had become a state. Standing on the statehouse steps in a pouring rain in Charleston, the young president began his speech of gratitude saying: "The sun does not always shine in West Virginia, but the people always do." It was a fitting tribute to the people who had voted for him in the 1960 primary election, showing the world a Catholic could win in a place known for its religious intolerance. That may have been West Virginia's finest hour.

President Kennedy was known, in part, for his anti-poverty programs. In the dismal coal mine communities of the Mountain State, the walls in almost every home were plastered with pictures of Jesus Christ, United Mine Workers President John L. Lewis and U.S. President John F. Kennedy. Was change finally coming to the Cumberlands? A new war would be underway soon in forgotten America—the War on Poverty—and the hollows of the hills would be giving up great stories for TV about a people whose lives were being altered dramatically.

Programs were on the move to enrich diets, improve education and retrain men and women for new jobs outside coal mining. People had hopes they might not only persevere, but prevail. CBS and its audiences loved the stories about people climbing out of poverty, because the reports revitalized the idea of the American dream. And

273

everybody believed in the American dream back then, way back then.

The network sent Charles Kuralt to do documentaries like his 1964 *Christmas in Appalachia*, an hour-long spectacle about the despair of poor families unable to buy food, much less toys for their kids at Christmastime. That made a lot of people mad. How dare Kuralt come down here and make fun of us?

Kuralt was simply being honest, reporting what was in plain sight. My own reports as a freelancer for CBS reinforced the gross reality of the hard times in the region, a brutal realism that led to my getting hired as a CBS Correspondent in New York. Amen!
But the emboldened movement to wrench the poor out of their awful plight was short-lived. Kennedy was assassinated, and President Johnson's War on Poverty was overshadowed by another war in a distant place thousands of miles away. Vietnam would become the new cause célèbre, a mammoth fad made for TV.

America's attention had shifted in a New York minute from my homeland to the rice paddies of South Vietnam. The shift occurred just as I started in big-time media at CBS. When I volunteered for Vietnam in 1969, CBS gave me the chance to cover the first ever television war.

Nobody wanted to look at the poor anymore. To do so and do nothing challenged the observer's humanity. So the new vogue was to watch how America was going to crush Communism right in front of our eyes on TV. The Vietcong, not scarcities and deficiencies at home, were the new enemy.

That war was as significant to me as it was to my home state, and I suppose that's why I return to the nation's experience with the war as I contemplate the status of West Virginia. Americans applauded President Johnson and the war in the early years, when he dropped millions of tons of bombs on Hanoi and down the Ho Chi Minh trail to smash the bad guys.

Americans, born of revolution and bred in almost constant conflict, love wars—short wars. Americans love to kill overseas. That's what we do for a living. Here at home, we kill off each other at alarming rates. We love our guns, and we use them with great effectiveness. But we tire easily when just cause peters out, leaving us with mind-dulling details, like how to explain all those deaths to Mom and Dad.

> *Then conquer we must,*
> *When our cause it is just,*
> *And this be our motto:*
> *"In God is our trust."*
> —Francis Scott Key, "The Star Spangled Banner"

When the boys started coming home in body bags on TV, we didn't like that picture very much. We turned away in disgust. Nobody likes to watch when America is deep-sixed. We just won't put up with that. No matter how many bombs and how many American lives, the Vietnam War ended in a humiliating defeat for America. So, too, the War on Poverty.

All people in Vietnam came under the control of Communism, and people in Appalachia continued to find themselves saddled with ignorance and deprivation. Attention was not returned to them by the media and Washington, and the blue bloods prospered by keeping things just as they were. Thus in 1968, the American dream died in Appalachia. "Time can bring you down … bend your knee ... break your heart ... have you begging please" (Eric Clapton, "Tears in Heaven").

It is true the Mountain State at times can be found in the blue on Election Day. Congressman Nick Joe Rahall and both U.S. Senators count themselves as Democrats. But peer just beneath the patina of party and you will find a bunch of crypto-Republicans masquerading as progressives. I know Senator John D. "Jay" Rockefeller, knew him and personally filmed him when he intrepidly changed his party affiliation from Republican to Democrat at the Kanawha County Courthouse in the early '60s.

Rockefeller overcame his carpetbagger status to serve West Virginians well while realizing his own enormous political aspirations. He camped out in a mountain hollow to help the poor and disadvantaged, picking up where the Kennedys left off in efforts to lift entire generations out of poverty and hopelessness. He rubbed shoulders with coal miners and bemoaned their deaths from black lung disease and the heedlessness to safety by coal companies intent on raping the land for the ancient and cursed mineral that bound their colliers in virtual servitude.

Then, in 2012, Rockefeller placed himself at great risk of becoming an illustrious statesman and a former U.S. Senator. He violated a cardinal rule, broke the 11th coal country commandment: Thou shalt not speak ill of coal. In a stunning speech on the Senate floor that instantly placed him among the highly honorable politicians dwelling in the pages of Kennedy's *Profiles in Courage*, Rockefeller dropped a bomb on West Virginia's vital coal industry. Coal is yesterday's energy, Rockefeller implied. There is no turning back the hands of time, he said. In one fateful act, he took to the Senate floor to oppose an effort to block an Obama administration rule targeting mercury emissions from coal-fired plants and, in so doing, he managed to buck

276

his colleagues in the state delegation, stick it to the coal companies and signal his political intentions not to run again for the Senate. It was Rockefeller's finest hour. But he joined the ranks of those who try to warn West Virginians only to be savaged by citizens who do not want to hear the warnings. I am one of the warners. So was my fellow investigative reporter Al Gore.

This is the state that denied Al Gore the presidency by voting for George W. Bush. It is opposed to new taxes and to gun control while combating freedom of choice for women and being anti-union to the core. Imagine a place that made its bones through the once-powerful United Mine Workers Union now embracing the tenets of extremism. Labor organizers are denounced as Communists, while pro-choice people are baby killers.

Tolerance cannot be the state's foundation. Unfortunately this is an outpost marking time, a place much maligned, and for good reason. Carl Sandburg wrote this in his narrative poem *Chicago*: "On the faces of women and children I have seen the marks of wanton hunger." If he had been writing about West Virginia, his words would have warranted equal consideration. One doesn't need university knowledge to see deaths from suicide and drug overdoses are on the rise. My cousins who care for the dead tell me it is so. My travels down the country roads show me we are retreating rapidly into the insular and self-protective world of a culture of poverty.

Appalachian parents hold high aspirations for their children's educational and occupational success. Those who can afford it send their offspring to fine schools outside. Then they tacitly and without shame forbid the children to come back home. Parents do not wish on their kids the travails and weaknesses of the region. They needn't worry. Most of the schooled stay away by design, rejecting their background.

The brain drain may be unprecedented. Those who would be reasonable are voting with their feet, leaving behind the wholesale lack of opportunity. They have been departing the state in droves. An average of 12,337 residents per year between 1950 and 2010—gone. That's 1,045 per month, 241 per week, and 34 per day. Imagine one person packing up and leaving the Mountain State every 42 minutes of every day, and you will have an appreciation of just how desperate people are to get out. The eastern panhandle of the state, close to Washington, D.C., is enjoying an increase in population. Overall, though, since 1950, almost 40 percent of the population, or a quarter of a million, have simply vanished from the population lists.

When I was young I couldn't wait to leave West Virginia. Now, as I get older, I value every day of my return. The magnificent rocks and hills, they soothe me. The majestic rivers and streams, they console me. The lush landscapes, they ease my pain. Surely I will live out my days here, at one with nature and her eternal reward. I am already immersed in my own history.

On the Internet I am listed as a famous West Virginian. Others from the state are listed there, too. That is the problem. Jerry West is *from* West Virginia. Senator John D. "Jay" Rockefeller is *from* West Virginia. So, too, Pearl Buck, the Pulitzer Prize and Nobel Prize winning author, *from* West Virginia. The late Senator Robert Byrd; Nobel Prize winner John Forbes Nash Jr.; Brigadier General Charles "Chuck" Yeager, first to break the sound barrier, all *from* West Virginia. They are not *in* West Virginia. They are *from* West Virginia.

My sister, Sharon Rabel Lewis, 67, and my brother, Douglas Rabel, 79, left long ago, never to return. Doug may die in exile. So may Sharon. They are not the only ones. West Virginians Cyrus Vance and Booker T. Washington never came home to stay.

Being *from* West Virginia is a vocation with occupational hazards and rewards. The benefits offered outside are legend: diversity, brand new peaks to be climbed, great opportunities abounding, the exciting environment in high society that encourages the pursuit of happiness, all the things that could be in my home state. These are the reasons famous people are *from* West Virginia and why they stay away.

Your zip code shouldn't limit your horizons. It shouldn't, but it does. Thank God for Mississippi, a state that ranks below West Virginia on many fronts. After a half-century abroad, I have come home to defy the odds. I have put aside the pleasures and prospects denied me here.

> *A prophet is not without honour, but in his own country, and among his own kin, and in his own house.*
> —Mark 6:4

No bands are playing; no welcome home signs have been posted anywhere. Such is the odd curiosity about this place. It is okay to be *from*, but don't try to come home. Thomas Wolfe addressed that issue.

A territorial spotlight shines on you if you are out there beyond the borders. "Look who's from West Virginia," is the preoccupation of those who won't or can't get out. *If only I could take my leave*, is the worry of those here who are trapped and longingly lust for the status of immigrant in some other location. They point with pride to the outlanders who've made it. They claw to join the ranks of the émigré.

279

And there is a kind of resentment here for the few successful ones who wish to make re-entry. Resentment bound up in bafflement over why on earth anybody would want to come back here. Stay away and let us bask in your glory. We have no place for you here. Your intransigence belies our great "get out" goal. *Sal si puedes*, escape if you can, seems to be the prime dictum, not to be disobeyed.

So my life now is one of self-imposed isolation. I have folded myself up among my Rabel Mountain roots with no regrets. But I would be less than honest if I denied that I am tortured by the realization that nothing much has changed here since I punched out. We are not in the NFL. The big leagues are elsewhere, not here. No vibrant, bustling international airport beckons. We still rely on the treacherous old Yeager Field, now the John D. "Jay" Rockefeller Airport to land on, if lucky. How sardonic that Rockefeller, the heir to a vast fortune, allowed his name to be inscribed on that low rent, outmoded landing field. Let Yeager/Rockefeller Airport, West Virginia's WW II era relic, symbolize the insidious boondocks we are in still. And let those who nixed the construction of a new, modern airdrome stand for all those here committed to retrograde. It is an appalling insight.

"Tell someone who cares," you say. "Rabel's return is irrelevant. *'Baise-moi!'* as the French put it. We can get along without you. We've done so for fifty years, thank you very much."

The profit of staying away is upon me now. Others from here who have chosen refugee status seem clairvoyant to me, relaxed and happy in their outwardness. Too bad they can't or won't come home. Farmstead is not in the cards.

I am satisfied, though, in living out my destiny here. Advantages of my bucolic surroundings seem preferable to the entanglements of modernity. Old ways and fundamental beliefs comfort me. They will prop me up in the time that remains.

If puzzlement is a problem for you still in understanding why on earth a country boy would want to come back to his country, here is more. There is in my replantation my long held view that no one should be left in the lurch. By reintegrating myself, I hope to satisfy my unyielding longing to be of service. And the preparation for service is bountiful in my long experience in the outland. To speak bluntly, my hope is to join others here who are striving to end the hardship of fellow West Virginians who do not know what traps them. I will assist in springing upon them the possibilities that define a globe they have never known nor wished to know.

Despite generations of tolerance of coal mining—a demeaning industry—for survival, folks in my neck-of-the-woods should be helped to make a swift conversion to a state with multiple businesses they can count on. Through my writing, I believe I can help them do that. West Virginia is bursting with natural resources other than coal that can be exploited and, in the doing of it leave the rest of the world intact. In a backward state yet to be introduced to meritocracy, new leaders can be elected to end a system of corruption and parochialism. I believe I can help bring that new day to pass.

In all ways and in all places on our shrinking planet, there is important work to be done. I have done my work on the outside. Now it is time to carry out my reason for existence back here on mother earth.

These things and more vitalize my underground cause, my private hope. My passion, my war cry: Commit to advancement and development, change because you must. "I am the grass. Let me work."

The End

About the Author

Ed Rabel, an Emmy Award-winning broadcast journalist and author whose reporting experience spans five decades of world-shaping events, is today a highly-respected strategic communications counselor and adjunct professor of journalism at The Edward R. Murrow College of Communications.

For more information email the author at:
rabeledward@yahoo.com

Find more books from Keith Publications, LLC At

www.wickedinkpress.com
www.dinkwell.com
www.dreamsnfantasies.com

CPSIA information can be obtained at www.ICGtesting.com
Printed in the USA
BVOW020921201112

305473BV00002BB/1/P